Mental Models
for Managers

1 7 JUN 2024

George Boak is a training consultant who has worked closely with managers at all levels from a wide range of companies in both public and private sectors. Before becoming a consultant he was the Programme Director for the Northern Regional Management Centre from 1987–1995.

David Thompson is Head of the Flexible Management Learning Centre, Newcastle Business School, University of Northumbria at Newcastle.

Mental Models for Managers

Frameworks for Practical Thinking

GEORGE BOAK AND
DAVID THOMPSON

C

CENTURY
BUSINESS

© George Boak and David Thompson 1998

George Boak and David Thompson have asserted their rights
under the Copyright, Designs and Patents Act, 1988,
to be identified as the authors of this work

This edition first published in the United Kingdom
in 1998 by Century Ltd
Random House, 20 Vauxhall Bridge Road,
London SW1V 2SA

Random House Australia (Pty) Limited
20 Alfred Street, Milsons Point, Sydney,
New South Wales 2061, Australia

Random House New Zealand Limited
18 Poland Road, Glenfield,
Auckland 10, New Zealand

Random House South Africa (Pty) Limited
Endulini, 5a Jubilee Road, Parktown 2193, South Africa

Random House UK Limited Reg. No. 954009

A CIP catalogue record for this book is available from the British Library

Papers used by Random House UK Limited are natural,
recyclable products made from wood grown in sustainable forests.
The manufacturing processes conform to the environmental
regulations of the country of origin.

ISBN 0 7126 7898 0

Typeset by MATS, Southend-on-Sea, Essex
Printed and bound in Great Britain by
Mackays of Chatham PLC, Chatham, Kent

Companies, institutions and other organizations wishing to make bulk
purchases of any business books published by Random House should
contact their local bookstore or Random House direct:
Special Sales Director
Random House, 20 Vauxhall Bridge Road,
London SW1V 2SA
Tel 0171 840 8470   Fax 0171 828 6681

Contents

*A detailed list of contents for this section of the book is to be found at the end of the introductory chapter on pp. 16–18.

Foreword

This book is for everyone who works with other people and is interested in reaching a better practical understanding of themselves and others.

Practical understanding is based on, and builds up through, the mental models we develop of ourselves and other people, of how to achieve results and of how things work.

For many years we have worked with managers and professionals on programmes of self-development and change. Our role as consultants and trainers has sometimes been to suggest changes or to help others implement them, but more often it has been to support individuals, to challenge preconceptions, and to introduce ideas which have helped our clients to develop their own ways of thinking, feeling and acting.

It has become apparent over the years that some of the models we have used in this process have been more powerful than others, and that some models have more impact if they are used in one way rather than another. These observations form the basis of this book.

In reaching this point of sharing how these models can best be used, we are indebted to more people than there is space here to acknowledge. Many of our models are original, but many more are based on the work of others, which we have borrowed in our practice and in this book. These originators are credited in the text at the appropriate point, but a general acknowledgement and thanks is due to them all. Without the faith, patience, intelligence and sometimes resilience of a great many clients in a number of organizations, we would not know which models are most effective, or how best to use some of the models. Despite the roles we occupied in working with them, it is sometimes hard to say who learned more from whom. Colleagues with whom we worked have also, through word and deed, contributed to our thinking about these models. There are too many people to name, but the staff of the Northern Regional Management Centre – and in particular Mac Stephenson – have guided and helped us to a great extent.

Heartfelt thanks, too, to our partners, Lindsay and Krysia, for the support and understanding that was needed for us to learn about and develop these models in the first place, and then to summarize and present them in the pages that follow.

George Boak
David Thompson

1. Introducing Mental Models

We all have a need to make sense of the world around us, in particular the situations in which we live and work. We need to understand what is important and what is not, and to be able to identify causes and effects with a certain amount of confidence. We all use mental models to understand how the world works, and these mental models have a profound effect on our behaviour.

John Berger says that:

> The way we see things is affected by what we know or what we believe. In the Middle Ages when men believed in the physical existence of Hell the sight of fire must have meant something different from what it means today. Nevertheless their idea of Hell owed a lot to the sight of fire consuming and the ashes remaining – as well as to their experience of the pain of burns.

Peter Senge sees the activity of working with mental models as a path which can lead to more effective organizations:

> Mental models can be simple generalizations, such as 'people are untrustworthy', or they can be complex theories ... But what is most important to grasp is that mental models are *active* – they shape how we act. If we believe people are untrustworthy, we act differently from the way we would if we believed they were trustworthy.

As Senge observes, many of our mental models may be unconscious, unspoken assumptions, and in order to see the world more clearly we need to surface and examine them.

Some models, however, are designed specifically to help us to make good sense of the world. The map of the London Underground, for example, represents a complex and messy reality in a simplified form that is easy to understand and use.

This book contains a variety of mental models that we have used as consultants and trainers over a number of years. The models have helped practising managers and professionals to become more effective – in some cases mapping out territories that were new and unexplored, in others challenging existing, unhelpful preconceptions.

Meaningful learning for adults is often more to do with seeing the world differently, or *reframing* it, than it is about learning new facts or theories. We often learn most by restructuring our familiar models of the world.

We include here a selection of what we have found in ten years of this type of work to be the most useful mental models – the ones which have provided the most leverage in helping people to understand and manage situations effectively. The most effective models, the ones which have had most impact on ourselves and on others, are often – although not always – the simplest.

We have grouped the models under five broad headings:

Managing Self
Leading and Managing
Change
Strategies and Structures
Achieving Results

There are overlaps between these categories, and cross-references between the models. The final section of the book sets out an index of different projects or activities and the relevant models in each case.

This is not an exhaustive compendium of useful mental models, and many of the people with whom we have worked have gone on to develop variations of these models, or crafted new insights of their own. There are a number of common types of model, and understanding the basic structures can help people to construct useful original models for themselves.

Simple assumptions, beliefs and values
These are perhaps the most common mental models. They may be highly specific to a situation, or they may be generalized: Senge's example, above, that 'People are untrustworthy' is a very broad belief of this type. More specific forms might include: 'People in the marketing department can't be trusted' or 'Customers who make complaints are usually just trouble-makers.' These simple mental models have an obvious effect on our behaviour: one person sees a customer who needs help; another sees a troublemaker.

These are personal examples – although they are beliefs that might be adopted and promoted by groups of people. Leaders of organizations increasingly put more stock by statements of positive corporate values, such as: 'The customer is always right' or 'Our main aim is to exceed customer expectations'. These value statements are intended to influence the culture of the organization, and to have a clear positive effect on the behaviour of employees.

In fact these value statements can often be used to demonstrate the difference between what Chris Argyris has called 'espoused theory' (what people say they believe in) and 'theory-in-action' (the values that appear to drive their behaviour). A company may have an inspiring list of positive corporate values, placing a high priority on meeting customer needs, whilst their employees and systems actually treat customer needs as secondary to the convenience of the company. In other words, the real models are quite different from those in the value statement.

Peter Senge is one of a number of writers who believe it is important to uncover and discuss the real values and beliefs that influence our behaviour, and the behaviour of groups within organizations. Limited and negative mental models will always hold back progress and development.

Some of the models in this book are based on simple assumptions, values and beliefs. Examples of beliefs we hold in common, as consultants and trainers, include:

- People are able to develop and change themselves, their skills, their knowledge, their attitudes, their performance.
- On the whole, working co-operatively with others is preferable to being in conflict or competition with them.

Such beliefs and values have had an effect in shaping our professional approach and naturally have also had an influence on the contents of this book.

We have also found that some models in this book challenge common (and often deeply held) beliefs of many of the clients with whom we have worked. Where it appears relevant to do so, we discuss these conflicts in the text.

Checklists
Some of the simplest models take the form of lists. These can be,

for example, lists of skills needed for a particular job, or of activities or functions that must be carried out. One of the earliest written models of management, by Henri Fayol, set out a list of functions that a manager must perform (one variation was: 'forecasting, planning, organizing, staffing, directing, co-ordinating, controlling, reviewing and budgeting'). Even earlier models, before the rise of 'management' as a role, aimed to list the key attributes of successful leaders.

These list models turn into true checklists when they set out reminders of the different activities that a person should perform in order to be effective in a particular role – for example, when chairing a meeting, carrying out a recruitment interview, making a presentation, conducting an appraisal, etc.

The value of this type of model, generally, is that it provokes consideration of the range of factors that must be taken into account, or the range of activities that must be performed. Checklists remind us not to concentrate all our energies on only one or two areas, but also to pay attention to the whole spread of relevant factors.

Checklists have a very simple format, but as they become more sophisticated, they may turn into other types of model – flow diagrams, cycles, or polar opposites.

Polar opposites
Polar opposites are formed by defining two ends of a spectrum. They may be used to indicate a basic choice between alternatives – an 'either ... or' model, a tug-of-war between competing options. They may arise from defining a pair of contrasting types, and then acknowledging that there are some cases which will lie somewhere on the continuum between the two.

For example, an early model of two contrasting leadership styles was that of the autocratic leader and the democratic leader. Initially the model was made up of a list of characteristics of each type of leader. This simple approach was then developed to establish a continuum, with at one end extremely autocratic leadership behaviour, and at the other extremely democratic behaviour, with a range of identifiable points in between.

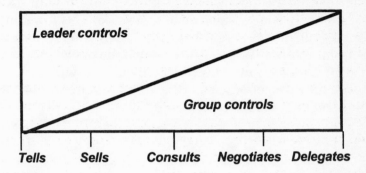

Autocratic   **Democratic**

Leader controls

Group controls

Tells   Sells   Consults   Negotiates   Delegates

Leadership styles
Based on Tannenbaum and Schmidt, 1973.

This model is obviously more sophisticated than the two simple categories, which reduced all the finer variants of behaviour into a choice between autocrat and democrat. Finer shades of meaning can be applied to particular behaviours. In addition, the model focuses on behaviour rather than on types of leader – so I might behave in a more democratic fashion in one situation – negotiating targets with my team – and a more autocratic fashion in another – selling them a proposal I want them to carry out.

For more on leadership styles see model 26 on p. 82.

Graphs and Charts
These are common types of model, usually employed to represent the changing relationship of one thing to another. A common usage is to show changes over time – costs, turnover or profits over a certain period, for example. Useful examples later in this book are the learning curve (see model 22), which shows the shape of improvement in skill as time passes, and the product life cycle (see model 53), which shows the likely shape of sales over the life of a product, while bar charts (see model 66) can be used to schedule project activities.

Some graphs are a development of polar opposite models. For example, the leadership styles model above can be developed in this way.

'Autocratic' is translated as 'Concern for Task Achievement', and 'democratic' as 'Concern for People'; the model can be represented as a straight-line continuum – an 'either . . . or' model – or by bending the line to create a 'both . . . and' model, a graph relating a concern with task to a concern with people. So, a leader may have a high concern for task and a low concern for people (1:9) or vice versa (9:1) – the classic ends of the simple continuum. Alternatively, a leader may trade one off against the other (5:5), or somehow achieve a high concern with task and a high concern with people (9:9). (Blake and Mouton, 1964, 1985.) For more on this, see model 26.

Task   **People**

'Either . . . or' model: concern for task *or* concern for people

Task

1.9   9.9

5.5

1.1   9.1

                                         People

'Both . . . and' model: concern for task *and* concern for people

These 'both . . . and' models can be valuable in a wide range of situations, particularly to transform conflicts within organizations that have built up around 'either . . . or' positions. When two groups are contesting the aims and purposes of projects or initiatives, and settling into an 'either . . . or' confrontation, the 'both . . . and' model may be a way of identifying synergies – or at least useful compromises.

Two-by-two matrices
These are very common in management education and training. Closely related to graphs, they are used to express the relation-

ships between two separate but connected factors.

For example, a common problem experienced by people who have difficulty in managing their time effectively is that they confuse the separate but connected factors of urgency and importance. An issue may be very urgent, but not very important. Another issue may be important but not very urgent. A third issue may be both important and urgent, whilst a fourth may be neither urgent nor important. A simple two-by-two matrix can illustrate this, and lead to the first steps in (a) allocating specific issues to each of these categories; and (b) formulating appropriate responses for issues in each of these categories.

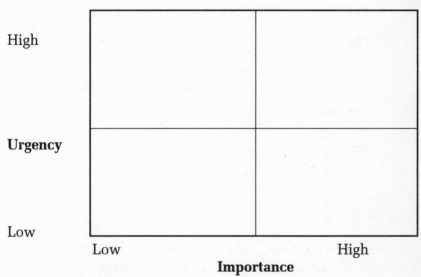

Importance

Urgency and importance

The value of two-by-two models is generally the way in which they demonstrate the effects of a simple relationship between two different factors. In this example, for instance, the degree of urgency of an issue only tells us about one dimension of its priority. Something might be very urgent – but of such low importance that we may decide to do nothing about it, and let the deadline pass. Something may not be at all urgent – but of such high importance that we decide to start working on it now.

A variation of this type of model is the three-by-three matrix, which has high, medium and low scales. We have included a number of matrix models in this book. For more information on this specific model see model 10.

Systems and flow diagrams
These usually represent a sequence of events, often indicating cause and effect. Flow diagram line models are used to represent the ways systems work within organizations, and can provide good visual images of what may be complex processes.

For example, the control loop model shows a typical pattern of production, measurement and correction. The common simple metaphor is of a thermostat in a heating system, which assesses the temperature against a standard and sends messages to the boiler to adjust the actual temperature if necessary.

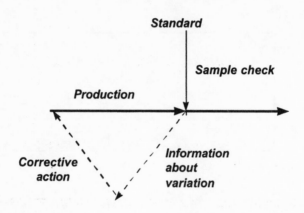

The control loop

In complex systems these diagrams can help by focusing attention on the most important aspects of the system. The control loop is a very common part of all production systems. Managers can question every aspect of the process set out in the diagram. Is the standard correct? Is the tolerance too wide or too narrow? Are we checking the sample at the right times? Is the sample too large/too small? Is the information about variations being received accurately? At the right time? Is corrective action carried out as quickly as possible? And so on.

Sometimes systems diagrams can illustrate quite clearly where systems are malfunctioning, and the expected pattern of cause and effect is shadowed by another, unintended sequence of behaviours. For more on this see models 67 and 68 on p. 185.

Ladders and pyramids
These diagrams are usually used to represent progression from

lower to higher levels. They are often helpful in distinguishing between different' stages, and in indicating a sequence of progression.

This example shows the key stages of developing a skill.

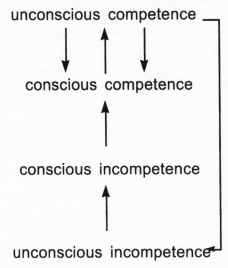

Levels of competence

In the beginning, we are in a state of *unconscious incompetence*: we are so unaware of the skill area, we do not know that our behaviour is incompetent.

If we are made aware of this, we rise to a state of *conscious incompetence*. Our performance may be little better than it was before, but at least we are aware of a shortcoming, or a development need.

With practice, with the acquisition of new skills and knowledge, our performance improves to the point where we might say we have become competent – but we are conscious of what we are doing to be effective.

With more practice, much of what we have been doing is internalized and becomes second nature to the extent that we do it unconsciously.

This is the simple ladder, moving only in one direction – upwards. The downward arrows represent a warning. Every now and again it may be useful consciously to check our performance, in case bad habits have crept in or the world around has changed. Otherwise the danger is that we may become incompetent without realizing it: we go right back down the snake to a state of unconscious incompetence.

For more information see model 21 on p. 69.

Cycles

Some sets of activities are cyclical: one event follows another in a regular pattern. The functions of management, which first appeared as a list of: forecasting, planning, organizing, staffing, directing, co-ordinating, controlling, reviewing and budgeting, were later to appear as a cycle of planning, organizing, directing and controlling, with information from the control phase feeding into the next round of plans.

The most valuable cycle model we have used is the learning cycle model designed by Peter Honey and Alan Mumford. This builds on work by David Kolb to identify the different types of activity that people need to undertake in order to develop skills, and is a particularly useful framework to support experiential and work-based learning.

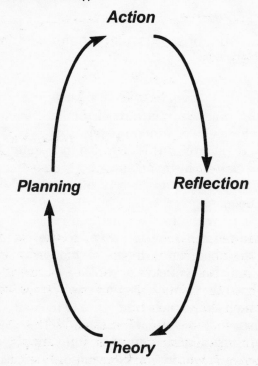

The learning cycle

The value of most cycle models is that they identify different activities or functions; they indicate the causal links that are (or should be) found; and they have a continuing dynamic. In the learning cycle, the first round of Action-Reflection-Knowledge-Planning naturally leads into a second round, and so on into a third. In the functions-of-management cycle, the control information naturally feeds into planning and into a new round of organizing, directing, controlling, etc. (See models 17 and 27.)

Venn diagrams
Sometimes it is important to express interactions between factors – as we saw above in the two-by-two matrices. For example, in a strategic alliance or a partnership, the two parties will be concerned with projects where they will benefit. We can see there might be three categories: projects where party A will benefit, projects where party B will benefit and projects where they will both benefit. A Venn diagram can illustrate this simply and quickly:

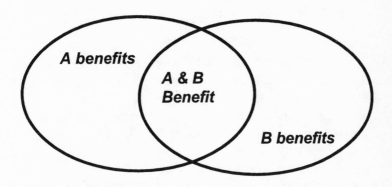

Overlapping benefits

This very simple model can help people to decide on priorities for action: for example at an early stage in a relationship it may be wise to concentrate on areas of mutual benefit; throughout the relationship we might hope for a balance of benefits between the two parties.

A third component – or even a fourth and fifth – can be added to this model. In negotiating strategies, for example, a manager employed by party A would consider not only areas of benefit, but also the pragmatic aspect of what the company is able to achieve: this indicates viable offers or joint projects that can be proposed.

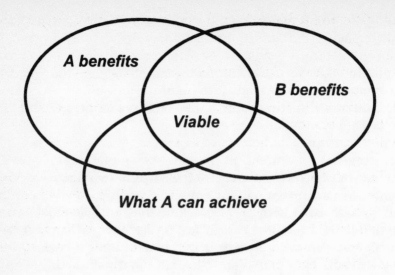

Viable projects
Based on Stumpf and Mullen, 1992.

The addition of the third explicit factor creates another four possible categories, which can be valuable in specific situations, in this particular model or in others represented in this way.

Other examples in this book of Venn diagram models include aspects of relevant competencies, the motivation to learn, and the functions of leadership (models 15, 19, 25 and 44).

Absolute and contingency models
In the early half of the twentieth century there were numerous attempts to define absolute rules for organizations and management: principles of organization were put forward that were expected to hold true in all circumstances; there were also ideas of styles of management that were supposedly correct for all situations. From the 1960s onwards, however, as the pace of change increased and as more serious study was carried out on organizations and management, it appeared to be the case that the best organizational structure and the best style of management depended on particular contingencies in each specific situation, and that it was not possible to give absolute answers.

Most of the models in this book reflect the need to consider contingencies. In the figure on p. 5 above, for example, a number of different styles of leadership are described. Which is the best one? According to the originators of the model, Tannenbaum and Schmidt, it depends on the circumstances, and in particular on:

- the maturity, skill, interest and motivation of the team members;
- the nature of the problem, the degree of time pressure, the type of organization;
- the manager's own skills and beliefs.

The most useful models, we have found, help us to make sense of our situation, and to take realistic decisions: they seldom presume to dictate reality, or to take the decisions on our behalf. In order to use them, we need to work with them, come to understand them and appreciate their benefits and limitations. They generally repay the effort.

REFERENCES

Argyris, Chris, *Overcoming Organizational Defences: Facilitating Organizational Learning*, Prentice Hall, 1990.

Berger, John, *Ways of Seeing*, BBC/Pelican, 1984.

Blake, R. R., and Mouton, J. S., *The Managerial Grid*, Gulf Publishing Company, 1964. *The Managerial Grid III*, Gulf Publishing Company, 1985.

Fayol, Henri, *General and Industrial Management*, Pitman, 1949.

Honey, Peter, and Mumford, Alan, *The Manual of Learning Styles*, Peter Honey, Maidenhead, 1988.

Kolb, David, *Experiential Learning as the Source of Learning and Development*, Prentice Hall, 1985.

Senge, Peter, *The Fifth Discipline: the Art and Practice of the Learning Organization*, Century Business, 1992.

Stumpf, Stephen A., and Mullen, Thomas P., *Taking Charge*, Prentice Hall, 1992.

Tannenbaum, R., and Schmidt, W. H., 'How to Choose a Leadership Pattern', *Harvard Business Review*, May/June 1973.

2. Using the Models

We have grouped the models on the following pages into broad themes, but there are many overlaps between them. The core models are presented in the first sections on self-awareness, personal effectiveness and self-development. We have seen issues of grand corporate strategy stand and fall on matters of individual personal ability – such as a person's self-confidence in the face of adversity, and the extent to which they can adapt to new circumstances.

Useful interpersonal models follow – and there are obvious overlaps here: the same models which I can use to understand myself, my capabilities and my ability to learn, I can also use to understand the same things in other people. But there are other issues here, too, of approaches to leadership and management, and to the ways in which people work together in groups and teams.

We have included only a small number of models on change, but each one has frequently proved its value in practice. It is still possible in some organizations – although fewer than was once the case – to avoid difficulties and challenges by observing the parameters and boundaries of one's strict responsibilities, and by maintaining the machinery and systems which worked well yesterday. Initiating change can bring about more challenges and difficulties, more hostility from what were once thought friendly quarters, than we might credit. Understanding how to manage change is an essential leadership skill.

We place an understanding of strategy and of achieving operational results on the outer rim of this collection of models – not because these are unimportant matters, for they are essential for the effective management of organizations, but because they build on and use an understanding of issues closer to the centre.

This is not to say that this book is designed to be read from front to back, in a linear sequence: it is not. You can dip into it at any point, following your particular interests. Where there are strong connections, you will see references to other models, and you may choose whether or not to follow up these links.

In the final chapter – Projects, Standards and Models – you will find an index linking particular models to common management projects and activities, such as expansion, team building, flexible working, re-engineering and discipline. This provides another way of tracking down the most relevant models. You will also find the models referenced here to the national UK Management Standards.

This collection contains a variety of models of different types. Most people will find some models with which they are familiar. Everyone will come across some models they have never previously encountered. Some models provide a new and unusual insight into situations; others provide a framework for identifying and analysing the component parts of an event, and will repay systematic and careful application.

The value of most of the models is in developing practical

understanding, and so they often require some mental effort, observation and persistence in order to apply them to the world around us.

Everyone has a slightly different way of learning, but we have found that a good way to approach a model is:

1. View the model with a detached mind, rationally – not on the basis of likes and dislikes. First make sure you understand the model and how it fits together.
2. Consider how you personally relate to each part of the model. If it is a model of individual activity, can you perhaps visualize yourself doing each part? Can you visualize yourself doing the whole model? If it is a model of how organizations or systems work, can you imagine how it applies to the organizations and systems with which you are familiar?
3. Consider how you feel about the model. What do you or might you feel about each part of the model if you were involved? What do you feel about the whole? Does it conflict with some of your beliefs and assumptions? Can you express those beliefs and assumptions?
4. Considering both your rational and emotional reaction to the model, do you think the model applies to you? Can you use it?
5. Practise using the model. Does it change the way in which you do things? The way in which people react to you? The results you achieve? Be patient – check the learning models 15–23, for the likely shape of your progress. If the model is complex there will be further references, to the originator, or to other examples of the model in practice, and you can follow these.

THE MODELS

Managing Self   19

Leading and Managing

Managing Self

Personal skills and abilities have always been important to effective performance, and much of our work as trainers and consultants has focused on areas of essential personal development. The functional skills – such as delegating, appraising, interviewing, marketing, strategic planning and so on – and the technical skills of the professional are extremely important in particular contexts, but underpinning them are some basic abilities. Professionals may be able to produce the solution that satisfies all the technical criteria, but if they are unable to make their case with flair and confidence they may have difficulty winning a hearing. Managers may know all the rules of how to delegate effectively, but if they are unable to assess what is important in a shifting set of circumstances they are unlikely to achieve success.

In this section of the book we concentrate on three areas of managing self that have proved to be essential:

1. *Self-Awareness*. This concerns gaining a practical understanding of oneself and one's own innate reactions and preferences, particularly under pressure. There are a number of mental models we have found to be of value in this context.
2. *Personal Effectiveness*. There are a number of key skills and competencies that can be used to help people achieve their goals in a wide range of circumstances.
3. *Self-Development*. The models we have used help people learn to cope with changing circumstances and changing demands on their skills and competencies.

Basic issues about managing self can be expressed as questions that managers have regularly raised:

- How can I handle difficult situations effectively and confidently?
- What do I want to achieve?
- How much of what I am can I change, and how much is part of my essential nature?

The models on the following pages have been helpful in answering these questions.

SELF-AWARENESS

Philosophies, religions and schools of psychology provide a range of answers to the deep questions of identity and self-understanding. People of different religious beliefs and those who have none have all benefited from concentrating on middle-range models for managing practical aspects of their affairs, regardless of their philosophy about the essential meaning of life.

The pressures of organizational life regularly present difficult changes and challenges. Whatever our values, we are all seeking success, and some degree of control over the situations in which we find ourselves. Having some understanding of ourselves – of our own drives, needs and repeated patterns of behaviour – can often help us to feel self-confident, and simple underlying beliefs about self-worth can have major effects on our lives. Self-doubt is corrosive. Self-confidence – and the appearance of self-confidence – is an important factor in achieving success and satisfaction. A balance is needed, however, for at the top end of the scale self-confidence shades into complacency and arrogance.

In this section there are six useful middle-range mental models for understanding self. They can be combined with the models in the rest of the book for managing particular situations.

1. Assertive Behaviour
2. Foundations of Assertiveness
3. Life Positions
4. Parent, Adult, Child
5. Drivers
6. Personality and Psychometrics

1. Assertive Behaviour

Many of the challenges confronting people at work are best faced with a mixture of honesty, straightforwardness and self-confidence. Everyday challenges include situations that many people find difficult, such as:

- criticizing someone, or making a complaint;
- giving bad news to someone;

- disagreeing and debating with other people;
- praising or complimenting someone;
- being on the receiving end of criticisms or complaints;
- being praised or complimented;
- making a request, making an offer, or negotiating;
- receiving a request.

Some of these situations contain clear seeds of conflict; in others the difficulty may be less obvious. But many people can feel awkward about receiving (or giving) praise and compliments, for example, and they behave in such a way that this awkwardness is communicated to others.

When faced with difficult situations, there are three possible ways in which we can behave: aggressively, assertively or submissively. The aim of those consultants and trainers who have written about assertiveness is to demonstrate why we should try to behave more assertively, and how we can do so. As consultants and trainers ourselves, we have found assertiveness models very powerful in helping people to examine their behaviour, and to change it.

Assertive behaviour, according to Madelyn Burley-Allen (1983, p. 2), is based on:

1. an active, rather than a reactive, approach to situations;
2. a positive, non-judgemental attitude towards both self and others;
3. standing up for one's own basic rights, without denying the rights of others;
4. communicating wants, dislikes and feelings in an honest and open manner, but without threatening others.

Assertive behaviour is essentially rational, but without denying or unduly suppressing much of the emotional side of one's nature. It is active and open about one's wants and feelings, but sensitive to the wants and feelings of others.

Aggressive and submissive behaviours are essentially emotional, or at least mediated much less by rationality.

It is not necessary (or personally desirable) to behave assertively in every situation, but it is generally desirable for people *to be able to behave assertively in difficult situations if they want to do so.*

The characteristics of the three modes of behaviour can be summarized as:

Aggressive	Assertive	Submissive
Stands up for own rights, usually in direct ways, but denies others their rights. Approaches issues in a win-lose frame of mind. Expresses emotions strongly.	Stands up for own rights without denying rights of others. Honest and open self-expression. Looks for win-win outcomes.	Avoids direct communication and avoids conflict. Reactive. Avoids expressing emotions – except perhaps frustration.
Effects: Achieves what one wants in the short term, and often experiences a sense of emotional release. In the longer term, likely to suffer retaliation from others, and to lose close relationships.	*Effects:* Maintains relationships with others, while at the same time making good progress towards achieving aims.	*Effects:* Succeeds in avoiding conflict in the short term. In the longer term, may fail to achieve aims, and likely to suffer loss of self-esteem and increasing frustration.

Using the model

This distinction between assertive, aggressive and submissive behaviours is the first of a number of models used when people are learning to become more assertive. It is helpful in drawing the first distinctions between different types of behaviour, but it is a reasonably well-known model, and in our experience you need to work on applying it to your own situation before it begins to add much value. Of course, as with all models of interpersonal behaviour, this three-way division simplifies reality in order to illuminate it, and in practice there are degrees of assertiveness that shade into aggression, and degrees that shade into submissiveness.

It is often easier to recognize the different modes of behaviour in others than in yourself, and without careful reflection and perhaps advice from other people whom you recognize as assertive, the immediate effect of using the model is simply to provide a whole new language for justifying existing patterns of behaviour.

The next steps in becoming more assertive are to work on the components of assertiveness, described on the following pages.

REFERENCE
Burley-Allen, Madelyn, *Managing Assertively*, Wiley, New York, 1983.

2. Foundations of Assertiveness

We defined assertive behaviour in the previous model: essentially it is active, open, honest and direct behaviour that stands up for our rights but does not deny the rights of others.

Recognizing assertive behaviour, and relating it to one's own situation, is a first step in learning to behave more assertively. Further steps can only be taken by building on the three foundations of assertiveness: ideas about rights and responsibilities; inner dialogue; and self-presentation.

Rights and responsibilities

The importance of 'rights' is at the heart of assertiveness: assertive behaviour stands up for our rights without denying the rights of others. So, if you are a diner in a restaurant and your soup is lukewarm you are *assertive* if you complain to the waiter in a clear and direct fashion and ask for the soup to be heated to the right temperature; *submissive* if you make do with what has been provided – a failure to stand up for your own rights; *aggressive* if you go on to abuse or insult the waiter or the establishment – a failure to respect the rights of the waiter, which could be described as the normal human right to be treated with reasonable respect and courtesy.

It is clear that it is important to have an idea of the rights and responsibilities of the parties in different situations. What rights and responsibilities do I have, for example, when it comes to giving critical feedback to members of my staff? What rights and responsibilities do they have in this situation? It is helpful to consider matters of rights and responsibilities in advance: they may become an issue for debate in themselves.

Inner dialogue

Inner dialogues are the streams of thought which affect our actions. If our inner dialogue in advance of a big presentation to senior managers is: *This is going to be really difficult. They're bound to try and catch me out. They gave Robinson a tough time at the last presentation. I've got to make sure I know everything, or this could be the last chance I get* . . . then the situation is seen as win-lose and the effect is likely to push us towards submissive, or towards aggressive behaviour.

There are two measures to take with inner dialogues:

1. become aware of them
2. challenge and change them where necessary

In practice, our initial inner dialogue may not be as coherent as it seems in the example above, but is likely to be simply a series of apprehensive feelings, mixed with emotional fight- or flight-messages. Becoming aware of inner dialogue means verbalizing the messages, either silently or out loud.

Challenging and changing the inner dialogue may mean examining the more extreme assumptions and attempting to lower the pressure they are applying: *Are they really going to try to catch me out? Just because Robinson had a tough time, does it really mean that I'll have one, too? And even if it goes badly, is this really the last chance I'll get?*

Negative inner dialogues can also be challenged by deliberately thinking positive thoughts, focusing on how everyone can benefit, and so improving our feelings of self-confidence.

Examining our inner dialogues can be a valuable way of examining the mental models we are using. If we see other people as hostile and aggressive, looking for opportunities to catch us out, we are likely to behave in aggressive ways towards them.

Self-presentation
The third foundation of assertiveness is the behaviour itself: even with sound ideas about rights and responsibilities, and a positive inner dialogue, we still need to be able to present ourselves with openness and honesty.

This can be done by working on ways of expressing ourselves, using patterns of speech that are effective and assertive, and also considering voice tones, facial expressions, and body language.

There are certain patterns of speech – or 'scripts' – that are effective in difficult situations, for example: 'I understand what you've said about the other demands on your time, but I want you to work on this area urgently'; or: 'With respect, I think you're mistaken there.' Both these scripts acknowledge the other person's point of view (or, to put it another way, their rights) but continue to stand up for your own viewpoint. Compare them with: 'Never mind about that, I want you to work on this area urgently'; or: 'And that's where you're wrong, of course' – both of which are more aggressive in content.

Of course, much depends on the style of delivery: assertive words and scripts may be undermined by a voice tone and body language that is either submissive or aggressive.

Using the model
This three-part model provides a very sound basis for being more assertive in difficult situations, and it can be built upon with practice and more ideas to help you to be more confident, relaxed and in control. Assertiveness can be seen as a key component of effective behaviour in a range of situations – including delegation, negotiation, presentations and interviews of various types, such as appraisal, recruitment, disciplinary, etc. Specific ideas of good practice in each of those areas can be added to the basic precepts of assertiveness – and in most cases there will be a good fit.

REFERENCES
Back, Ken and Kate, *Assertiveness at Work*, McGraw Hill, Maidenhead, 1991 (2nd edn).
Burley-Allen, Madelyn, *Managing Assertively*, Wiley, New York, 1983.
Stubbs, David R., *Assertiveness at Work*, Pan, London, 1986.

3. Life Positions

Transactional analysis provides a set of very useful models for understanding behaviour. These models are complementary to those of assertiveness (discussed in models 1 and 2) but they have the advantage of shedding light on areas where assertiveness does not venture.

Transactional analysis (TA) is a collection of ideas that originated with Eric Berne in the 1960s, and has been developed since then. Perhaps the best-known TA book is still Berne's

Games People Play, an amusing and in some ways quite instructive book, but one which we have found has little actual value in helping novices to gain a practical understanding of TA.

One of the two most powerful (and simple) models of TA is that of life positions. According to Berne, there are four basic life positions – attitudes which people adopt and act out concerning their self-worth and the value of others. He used simple and effective language to express high and low esteem:

		Not OK	OK
View of self	OK	I'm OK, you're not OK – compete, aggression	I'm OK, you're OK – co-operate, share
	Not OK	I'm not OK, you're not OK – avoid	I'm not OK, you're OK – submit to, concede

View of others

The first position, developed by a little baby in relation to its parents, is 'I'm not OK, you're OK' – an expression of the baby's dependence and helplessness compared to that of the parents. This position, according to Berne, in most cases then develops into one of the other three life positions.

The only truly positive life position is that of 'I'm OK, you're OK' – I feel good about myself and my self-esteem is high, and I also respect and regard you (other people) highly.

Working in a non-therapeutic context, we have found this model to be very effective when applied to people's attitudes towards particular situations – rather than attempting to use it to analyse their habitual attitudes (life positions) towards themselves and others. In specific situations, the 'I'm OK, you're OK' position has obvious connections with a positive inner dialogue, with respecting the rights of yourself and others, and thus with assertive behaviour – although it does not necessarily imply the level of activity and initiative associated with assertiveness.

In an organizational context, an 'I'm OK, you're OK' position does not imply a laissez-faire attitude towards behaviour, but it can lead to a beneficial separation of the behaviour from the individual.

Suppose I make an error in judgement in a business deal, and the company fails to make a sale. I can view the behaviour with some dismay and concern, and consider how I might avoid repeating this mistake, but I will (I hope) continue to regard myself as OK. In the long run this attitude will also remove (or at least dampen) the roller coaster of highs and lows that my self-esteem might experience if its position is based on the most recent success or failure.

Suppose a member of my team is causing problems for other team members through his disruptive behaviour. I will probably be better able to discuss the matter with him in a way that might lead to a resolution of the situation if I focus on the behaviour, rather than on the person himself. His behaviour is, in fact, causing the problem. If I can regard him with respect and esteem (in other words, as OK) I am more likely to be able to communicate effectively with him, and therefore manage him effectively.

Using the model
We have found that this model can provide good discipline when handling difficult situations – particularly those where a person has to come to terms with their own failure in some project or enterprise, or comes into conflict with another person. The natural tendency of many people in this situation is to transfer their bad feelings about the behaviour to the person himself. Your failure in a project can lead you to think 'I'm not OK'. Someone else's behaviour, at odds with yours, leads you to feel 'he's not OK'. These feelings are generally not helpful in managing the situation.

REFERENCES
Berne, Eric, *Games People Play*, Penguin, 1968.
Harris, Thomas A., *I'm OK You're OK*, Pan, London, 1969.
Stewart, Ian, and Joines, Vann, *TA Today*, Lifespace, Nottingham, 1987.

4. Parent, Adult, Child

Eric Berne, the originator of transactional analysis (TA),

identified three 'ego states' – Parent, Adult, Child – as 'psychological realities' within each person. He observed that at times his patients would behave as though they were reciting lessons they had learned from their parents, at other times as though they were still the uninhibited children they had once been. This structural analysis of personality into Parent, Adult, Child is the basis of much work in TA.

In a non-therapeutic context, as we seek models to understand behaviour in everyday interactions, the simple structural model provides a useful framework for answering some of our questions.

For example, suppose I am at my desk one sunny afternoon, looking down the list of tasks I drew up last night for completion today. A number of thoughts may pass through my mind, such as: *Do the easy one first . . . I'll just take the afternoon off . . . What a long list . . . Have I forgotten anything? . . . Do the worst thing first . . . It's already too late to do that one . . . I'll never get this done . . . What's the point? . . . Wasn't I supposed to ring someone else? . . . Why do I always draw up such long lists? . . . A cup of tea first, before I do anything . . .*

This jumble of thoughts, coming from a number of different standpoints, can be typical of situations where we have to make a decision but there is no immediate time pressure, or pressure to react to someone else.

In another situation – say where a member of our team is being criticized by a more senior manager – the thoughts may be fewer in number but more sharply contrasting: expressing a mixture of annoyance with the senior manager, protectiveness for our team member, but also anger with that team member, too.

Berne's framework of Parent, Adult, Child explains the origins of these thoughts, and gives an indication about how to manage them.

The Parent, according to Berne, is a set of behaviours, thoughts and feelings copied from our parents, or other authority figures we encountered early in life. There may be an emphasis on what a person (ourselves or someone else) should do. The Parent is divided into Nurturing Parent and Critical Parent, so there tends to be an emphasis either on protecting and caring (for someone else or ourselves) or on criticizing (again, someone else or ourselves).

The Adult is a set of rational, problem-solving thoughts and behaviours related to the here and now. There tends to be a concern with how things work, or how to achieve things.

The Child is a set of behaviours, thoughts and feelings replayed from childhood. The Child is divided into the Adapted Child and the Natural Child, so there tends to be an emphasis either on compliance with authority, or on free expression of feelings.

Events which occur around us in the here and now can trigger reactions from the Parent and the Child ego states in ways that may not be appropriate to the immediate situation. The thoughts that passed through my mind as I looked at my list of things to do are a mixture of Parent, Adult and Child, whereas the criticism of my team member has aroused both the Nurturing and the Critical Parent.

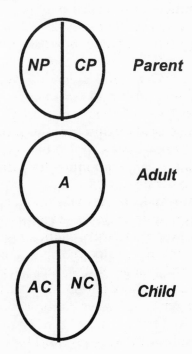

Using the model

This simple model is very valuable for becoming more aware that some of our deeply rooted, instinctive reactions to events may be patterned around thoughts and feelings that have a historical relevance for us, but may not be at all appropriate in specific current situations.

The behaviour of members of your team may arouse your Critical or Nurturing Parent, but it is unlikely to be appropriate to allow the Parent to regulate your behaviour towards them. Senior managers may arouse your Adaptive Child ego state, but again it is unlikely to be appropriate to allow your Child to govern your behaviour towards them.

The lesson is not to stay in the Adult state all the time (which is not possible) but to use the Adult to try to understand the origins and nature of our thoughts and feelings, and to monitor and correct any repeated discrepancies between the current situation and our reactions to it.

Transactional Analysis is a comprehensive and detailed approach to self-development: the Stewart and Joines text is an excellent source of further information.

REFERENCE
Stewart, Ian, and Joines, Vann, *TA Today*, Lifespace, Nottingham, 1987.

5. *Drivers*

Drivers are an idea used in Transactional Analysis closely linked to the of Parent, Adult, Child (as in model no. 4).

Some TA practitioners believe that there are a number of common Parent messages – or 'tapes' – playing to us, and that these strongly influence – or *drive* – our thoughts, feelings and behaviour through our Adapted Child. If we can detect these drivers we are in a better position to neutralize them and to base our thoughts, feelings and actions on more balanced assessments of the actual situations that face us.

The common drivers are:

1. *Be perfect:* the driver leads the Adapted Child in us to be anxious about making mistakes, and so we may become unnecessarily uncertain about committing ourselves to a decision.
2. *Hurry up:* the driver pushes the Adapted Child to do things quickly, and we may become needlessly anxious about delays.
2. *Please others:* the driver makes the Adapted Child anxious to please other people, and may lead us to be overdependent on the opinions of others.
4. *Try hard:* the driver encourages the Adapted Child to strive, to expend effort and determination – and as a result we may

become too concerned with the striving at the expense of the achievement.

5. *Be strong:* this driver encourages the Adapted Child in us to control its emotions, and may lead us to deny our feelings, or to blame them on someone or something else.

According to Stewart and Joines, each of us is likely to show all five of these driver behaviours at some time or another, but most people have one dominant driver, which has the greatest effect on their behaviour.

Drivers can be seen as the essence of some of our inner dialogues. For example, if I am considering a home improvement project, my inner dialogue may be concerned with absolutely accurate measurements – 'I must get this exactly right' – or about the very best materials and methods to use – 'I wonder if there's a better way of doing this – I must find out.' If I am recounting an anecdote, I may be overly concerned with the exact details of the story: my inner dialogue is 'You must get it right.' By now you will be able to work out which one of the five drivers is influencing my behaviour!

A dominant driver will affect a person's behaviour regularly and strongly. The other drivers may only have an occasional influence, perhaps in particular circumstances.

Using the model
You can use the model to detect driver behaviour in yourself (and other people), and you may then work to reduce the influence of the drivers over your Adapted Child.

Neutralizing a driver is a matter of establishing a positive message – one that contradicts the driver – in our inner dialogue.

Stewart and Joines recommend these positive messages:

Be perfect: You're good enough as you are.
Hurry up: Take your time.
Please others: Please yourself.
Try hard: Do it.
Be strong: Be open and express your feelings.

REFERENCE
Stewart, Ian, and Joines, Vann, *TA Today*, Lifespace, Nottingham, 1987.

6. Personality and Psychometrics

A common definition of personality is 'more or less stable internal factors that make one person's behaviour consistent from one time to another, and different from the behaviour other people would manifest in comparable situations' (Child). These relatively stable internal factors are generally known as 'traits'.

Let's look at three descriptions of a person:

1. He behaved charmingly.
2. He is a charming man.
3. He has more charm than she has.

In the first description 'charmingly' describes the behaviour, which may or may not be typical of the person. The second two descriptions imply that the behaviour *is* typical, that it has the more enduring characteristic of a trait. In everyday life we can often move quickly (sometimes too quickly) from commenting on behaviour to commenting on what we think are traits of the people themselves.

Personality profiling, also known as psychometrics, is an attempt to identify an individual's traits. Most profiles use self-assessment questionnaires and therefore depend to a degree on the accuracy of our self-image and on our understanding of the questions. The results may also be subject to deliberate bias – we may not be entirely honest, for example, if we are being assessed for job purposes.

Profiling tools typically use bi-polar scales of descriptive terms when producing results. We can plot ourselves more or less one way or the other. A well-known example is:

Introversion ◄─────────────────────────────────► Extroversion
quiet, has fewer friends, less active, serious-minded, conscientious, cold, inner-looking, shy   stimulus hungry, aggressive, unable to control feelings, warm, bold

Two well-established psychometric models of personality are Myers-Briggs and 16PF.

Myers-Briggs is derived from Jung's psychological types: there are four main scales:

←——————————————————→

E Extroversion	Prefer to *focus attention* on the outer world.	Prefer to *focus attention* on the inner world.	I Introversion
S Sensing	Tend to *look at things* in the present and on concrete information.	Tend to *look at things* in the future, looking at patterns and possibilities.	N Intuition
T Thinking	Tend to *base decisions* on logic and on analysis of cause and effect.	Tend to *base decisions* on values.	F Feeling
J Judging	*Deal with the outer world* through planning and organizing life.	*Deal with the outer world* through a flexible and spontaneous approach to life.	P Perceiving

The results of the Myers-Briggs test are given as one of sixteen broad profiles, for example ENTJ. A person with this profile could be described as logical, organized, structured, objective and decisive, a person who is action oriented, takes charge and provides structure.

The level of detail is enhanced by prioritizing the order of the four types, for example, rather than ENTJ a particular individual may be TEJN, where the thinking aspects are more significant than the extroversion aspects. Additionally, with the support of a good profiling counsellor, the basic profile can be considerably more detailed with reference to a person's actual experiences and behaviours.

The 16PF (Personality Factor) model has been based on large samples of behavioural data:

←——————————————————→

A	Reserved	Warm
B	Low intelligence	High intelligence
C	Affected by feelings	Emotionally stable
E	Accommodating	Dominant
F	Serious	Impulsive
G	Expedient	Conscientious
H	Shy	Bold
I	Tough-minded	Sensitive
L	Trusting	Suspicious
M	Practical	Imaginative
N	Forthright	Shrewd
O	Self-assured	Apprehensive
Q1	Conservative	Radical

Q2	Group dependent	Self-sufficient
Q3	Uncontrolled	Controlled
Q4	Relaxed	Tense

The above are the sixteen primary factors. The terms used have a number of shades of meaning: for example, Factor H, Shy, can also mean *restrained, withdrawn, careful, considerate.* The primary factors can be clustered in a large number of ways: for example, A+ Warm, F+ Impulsive, H+ Bold and Q2- Group-dependent together make up a secondary factor called extroversion.

Using the models

Most people now accept that our behaviour results from a mix of our traits, the situations we find ourselves in, and the social roles we are expected to play. An understanding of someone's personality can sometimes help to predict his behaviour, but it is not an entirely reliable forecast.

As consultants and trainers, we have sometimes used personality profiling to help managers and professionals who are undertaking a programme of personal development. A psychometric model can provide some structure for describing likes and dislikes, tendencies and preferences.

If you are interested in exploring this area further, either for a self-assessment or for using psychometric tools for assessing others, you might pursue the recommended reading below. Personality profiling is complex and is not to be treated lightly. Profiling tools need professional handling.

REFERENCES

Child, Dennis, *Essentials of Factor Analysis*, Cassell, 1990 (2nd edn).
For Myers-Briggs see:
Keirsey, David, and Bates, Marilyn, *Please understand me*, Prometheus Nemesis, 1984.
Myers, I. B., and McCauley, M. H., *Manual: a Guide to the Development and Use of the Myers Briggs Types Indicator,* Consulting Psychologists Press, Paolo Alto, CA, 1985.

For 16 PF see:
Cattell, R. B., et al, *Handbook for the sixteen personality factor questionnaire*, Institute for personality and ability testing, Champaign, Illinois, 1980.

PERSONAL EFFECTIVENESS

There has long been the idea that successful men and women have a core of qualities or characteristics that enable them to achieve success, no matter what vocation or project they pursue – and this core is sometimes known as *personal effectiveness*. It is pointed to in the biographies of great leaders and the myths that surround them. On a more modest scale, perhaps, it can be recognized in the people around us: this person has it – or seems to have it – whereas that person . . . no, we are not so sure about that person. When we try to define it, however, to describe in a little more detail what this person has and that person does not, the words often become vague and general, and opinions may diverge. Is it energy, initiative, decisiveness, charm, enthusiasm – or a mixture of all these things and more besides?

One component appears to us to be the self-confidence and self-understanding that the models in the previous section address. Another appears to be the ability to be reasonably objective in analyzing information. A third is the ability to achieve results.

Managers may ask – in relation to a particular situation, or more generally – what do I want to achieve? This is an area where, as consultants and trainers, we tread cautiously. We assume that people wish to be effective in their jobs (whatever that entails) and seek some kind of success (however they define this). This often involves them taking steps to gain more control over what they are doing, and clarifying exactly what it is they do want to achieve. Their aims can range from wanting to change the world – or at least their small corner of it – to wanting to lead a quiet life. As most of our clients select themselves, more of them have tended to want to achieve the former than the latter. However, some have undergone transformations part-way through the journey towards where they thought they wanted to go, and set off in another direction altogether. Some have settled into situations they encountered by chance along the way, which they found agreeable and satisfying. The planned destination seems in many ways less important than the business of establishing a purposeful direction.

The following models have been useful in addressing the area of the central skills that may help people to be effective in a wide range of circumstances:

7. Personal Competencies
8. SMART
9. Time Management
10. Managing Time: Urgency and Importance
11. NLP
12. Thinking Hats
13. Creativity
14. Circles of Influence

7. Personal Competencies

There have been numerous attempts down the centuries to identify the essential skills of great leaders – and more recently great managers. Since the 1970s a common approach has been to use psychological focus to identify behaviours that are characteristic of excellent performers, and then cluster these behaviours together into competencies.

George Klemp, one of the leading researchers in this field defines a competency as 'an underlying characteristic of a person which results in effective and/or superior performance in a job'. The competency movement builds on the work of David McClelland who, in the 1950s, identified different primary needs of individuals. More recently, McClelland and his colleagues have concentrated on identifying the specific behaviours exhibited by effective managers. Once identified, the behaviours are grouped into themed clusters. These clusters are the 'underlying characteristics', or competencies. The typical shape of a behavioural competency model, therefore, is a list of competencies, each with a number of key behaviours attached to it.

One example is the competency model for senior managers developed in the UK for the Management Charter Initiative:

Not all of the competencies in a model will be relevant for all managers all the time. The demands of the job, of the organization and of the specific situation will mean some competencies are required more than others at particular points in time (see model 15). It is important to remember that competencies are not valuable in themselves but only insofar as they help managers to achieve results. There may be contradictions between some of the competencies in a model – for example, some may indicate the importance of team work, while others may place a high value on independent action. Managers must use their judgement and initiative about when to behave in a particular way – in other words when to use a particular competency.

Strategic perspective
Key behaviours:
- works towards a vision of the future based on a strategic perspective;
- uses understanding of how different parts, needs or functions of the organization and its environment fit together;
- clearly relates goals and actions to the strategic aims of the business;
- takes opportunities when they arise to achieve longer-term aims or needs.

From: The Personal Competency Model for Senior Managers, Management Charter Initiative, 1993.

Competency models can provide a good format for expressing the general skills needed for personal effectiveness. Numerous in-company models have been created in recent years as an aid to appraisal, training and development.

The value of a competency model depends on three overlapping factors:

1. *Accuracy:* the extent to which it represents the actual competencies required for effective performance.
2. *Acceptability:* the extent to which it is acknowledged by its users as an accurate and helpful model: this depends partly on its accuracy, of course, but also on the way in which it has been derived and the way in which it is introduced to users.
3. *Accessibility:* the extent to which the model is easy to understand and to apply. It is possible for a model to be extremely accurate, and accepted by its original users, but to be difficult to access – often because it is too long and complex. Increasing the accessibility may mean simplifying it – and reducing the accuracy.

REFERENCES

The Personal Competency Model for Senior Managers is available from MCI, Russell Square House, 10–12 Russell Square, London WC1B 5BZ.

Klemp, G. O., Jnr, 'The assessment of occupational competence', report to the National Institute of Education, Washington, USA, 1980, cited in Boyatzis, R. E., *The Competent Manager: A Model for Effective Performance*, New York, Wiley, 1982.

McClelland, D., 'Testing for competence rather than for intelligence', *American Psychologist*, 28, 1973.

Spencer, L. M., and Spencer, S. M., *Competence at Work*, Wiley, 1993.

The best source of up-to-date information on company competency models is the journal *Competency*, published by IRS, 18–20 Highbury Place, London N5 1QP.

8. SMART

SMART is an acronym of the five desirable features of good objectives:

Specific: setting out clear and precise targets.
Measurable: quantifiable, such as sales and production targets.
Achievable: realistic – but only achievable if the individual

puts in a little extra effort to reach them.

Relevant: congruent with broader goals – such as, in the case of work objectives, those of the company or the department in which the person works.

Time-bound: the objective should include deadlines.

SMART objectives appear to have become more popular recently, perhaps with the increase in use of company appraisal and development schemes that include action plans.

The acronym acts as a good reminder of the characteristics of good objectives, and can help us to guard against directionless drift, or vague short-term aims. The logic of the model is such that:

- objectives should be written statements (otherwise it is difficult to be specific and measurable in respect of any but the simplest of targets);
- progress towards objectives should be reviewed (at appropriate points in time).

The simplest effective format for setting out SMART objectives is a three-column system, with space at the top for expressing the overall goal. As trainers, we use a version of this in A4 size, landscape orientation, for learning contracts and personal development plans.

GOAL:		
Objectives	Action plan	Review

In this format, both the objectives and the action plan should have as many attributes of SMART as possible (in some systems the second column is called 'Milestones' to emphasize this point). Particularly where it is difficult to set very specific, measurable objectives, it is useful to pay special attention to the specifics of the activities the person will undertake.

Using the model

In our experience the model works well when it is recognized as an aid to improving performance. You can use it on an individual level to clarify personal, work and learning objectives.

In some organizations, however, SMART has become part of a fetishism of objectives, and too much of the effort which could otherwise go into achieving results is diverted into writing out objectives, negotiating and renegotiating them, reporting on progress or lack of it, and so on. Most of the people involved in these processes acknowledge the unreality of them. Part of the problem in these situations is usually that SMART objectives have been allowed to proliferate to cover every aspect of operations (supposedly, at least, although there are often very important aspects of management that are not covered).

A good part of the solution – for organizations and individuals – may be to use explicit SMART objectives sparingly, targeting key areas for achieving improved performance.

It is not always really practical to set objectives with all five characteristics of SMART.

It should be possible (and it is always desirable) to set time-bound objectives – because a deadline triggers a review. And it should be possible to set relevant objectives – or ones that appear so at the time.

For 'Measurable' there are two schools of thought. One school emphasizes the importance of quantifiable targets for output – even if these targets are surrogate measures, or their achievement is not entirely within the control of the individual. The other school holds that in some areas of important managerial or professional activity results may be extremely difficult to quantify – but it is often valuable to make plans and set objectives in these areas. The results can be evaluated, judged or assessed largely on the basis of non-quantitative criteria.

For example, how do you measure a growth in your network of contacts? (See model 46.) There may be certain quantitative measures you could use as surrogates: for example, an increase in the number of committees on which you sit, an increase in the number of times you communicate with X, Y or Z, an increase in the number of joint ventures you undertake. But it will also be wise to make qualitative assessments of any growth, to ensure that these surrogate measures do not transmit a misleading picture.

Finally, when moving into new areas of activity, a lack of knowledge may mean you have difficulty in setting specific objectives that are in fact achievable. You may need to settle for broader aims at first – or set specific targets and allow yourself to amend them when you have been able to assess their achievability.

9. Time Management

Training in time management has for many years been a popular area, and we have worked with many organizations who have wanted to offer short time management courses for staff at all levels.

It was quite common to find that the people who attended these courses were suffering from the classic symptoms of poor time management: feeling that there were not enough hours in the day, suffering from the stresses and strains of overwork and inefficient working practices, committing the occasional dreadful mistake by trying to do something too quickly. What was not so common was consensus on the causes of these symptoms.

A classical top-down model of time management problems is that they are the result of inefficient or ineffective working habits on the part of the individual – and the solution is to adopt better methods of working, using 'to do' lists, time logs, etc. In other words, become more productive. This is a second reason why time management courses have been popular: the solution appears not only sensible, but also safe – whereas companies for some reason have been slow to sponsor courses called 'Persuasion Skills for Managers' or 'How to Manage Your Boss'.

In fact, individuals do often create many of their own time management problems, and lists and logs can be important tools in repairing the situation, but it soon became apparent to us that a slightly more sophisticated model of time management was necessary.

Time management problems are caused at three levels: the individual, the team and the system:

1. *Individual causes:* include wasting time on matters of low priority, while more important matters are neglected, and failing to organize tasks so that they can be completed in a

time-efficient way. Difficulty in prioritizing is a typical characteristic of the poor time manager at this level: who often has a clear grasp of the trivial, but has thought very little about the seriously significant issues.

2. *Team causes:* include frequent – often disruptive – demands on your time by the people immediately around you, including your boss. These demands may range from brief interruptions to the disruptive effects of dramatic changes in what is required from you from your boss or other colleagues.

3. *System causes:* often include lack of resources, which makes jobs larger or more difficult than they might otherwise be, and laborious organizational procedures, which consume and/or waste too much time.

Using the model

There is little value in using the traditional time management tools of better organization to address problems which have at their root team or system causes.

Problems that are caused by the behaviour of people around you can only finally be addressed by taking action to modify their behaviour, or to reduce its impact on you. Frequent interruptions, for example, are usually most disruptive either when we are trying to give a piece of work our undivided attention, or when we are trying to have a meeting with someone. It may be possible to divert the interruptions (close the office door), forestall them (check with people most likely to interrupt you before you try to begin a piece of work or start the meeting), avoid them (go and work somewhere else for a while, hold the meeting somewhere else), or rebut them (refuse to break off what you are doing when interrupted). Similarly, there are strategies for dealing with other kinds of team-based problem – such as the boss or colleague who constantly switches plans and priorities, the member of staff who regularly tries to delegate upwards, the unreliable colleague.

Team-based problems are generally more difficult to resolve than those that are individually based. With the latter, we often need to overcome our own habits and preferences, and our assumptions – often unfounded – about what is essential and what is not. With the former, we also have the habits, preferences and assumptions of others to contend with.

Problems that can be traced back to system causes are often even more difficult to resolve. To solve them we may need to make a successful case for a reallocation of duties or resources, or changes to systems and procedures: there is often serious resistance to proposals for change in these areas. As with some of the team-based issues, we may need to demonstrate the extent of the problem before our case will be taken at all seriously.

Time management problems, perceived as too much to do, or too much time wasted on matters which are later not followed through, or simultaneous conflicting demands.	Individual causes	Solutions: re-examine priorities and working habits; improve self-organization; identify main areas where time is being wasted; take action to relieve stress.
Time management problems may lead to mistakes, oversights and missed opportunities, and also individual stress and potential illness.	Team causes	Solutions: take action to modify the behaviour of the people concerned – train them to be more self-reliant, or more considerate of your needs.
	Systems causes	Solutions: make a case for systems to be changed.

The mental models of what is important and what is not often create and compound the time management problems people endure – because solving time management problems may mean making changes to working behaviours that are ingrained by habit and based on deeply held assumptions. Suggest to managers with an open-door policy to their staff that in order to solve their time management problems they should occasionally shut the door, and they are likely to reject the advice out of hand. Their model of good team leadership places much importance on the open door. But only if prepared to reconsider that model will they be able to make progress with their problem.

REFERENCES
See model 10. Many of the models in the section on Change (p. 117) are also relevant to solving team and systems problems.

10. *Managing Time: Urgency and Importance*

The most important resource of the busy manager is his or her own time. Of all the short training course topics, time management is one of the most popular.

Becoming a better manager of time involves being clear about what we want to achieve – about our objectives and their relative priority. One effective model for analysing priorities is the urgency/importance matrix. Any demand on our time – whether it is in response to a request from another person, or an activity we have initiated – can be prioritized in terms of its urgency and its importance.

Urgency and importance are sometimes confused: they are not the same thing. Urgency is indicated by the proximity of a deadline. When must the task be completed? Importance is indicated by the consequences of actions. What will be the results of doing – or not doing – the activity? Urgency and importance can be mapped against each other in a two-by-two – or as here in a three-by-three – matrix.

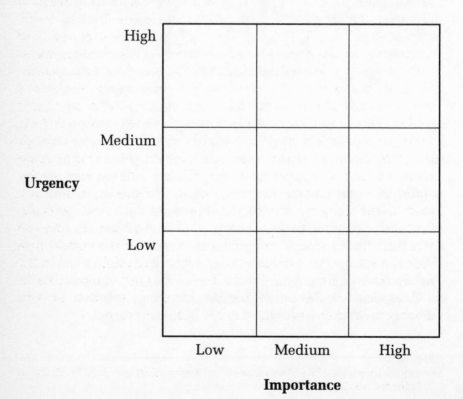

The natural tendency for many people is to concentrate on the more urgent matters, often at the expense of the important but not urgent ones. But to be effective, we should give more care, more thought – and therefore more time – to the more important matters.

A first step in achieving this is to review the tasks and demands facing us and establish the importance and urgency of each of them.

Using the model

You can use the model simply for managing your own time, or you can introduce it to your team as a means of clarifying and questioning group priorities. Demands on your time can then be logged on to the matrix. The different sections of the matrix can be given simple codes: a good working system is to call the high, medium and low importance columns A, B and C respectively. A very urgent high-importance task becomes a High A; a medium-urgency high-importance task is a Medium A; a low-urgency high-importance matter is a Low A.

Once you have analysed (and perhaps debated) the position of various demands on the grid, you should aim to find ways of reducing the amount of time you spend on matters of lower importance – the C column – however urgent they are, and increasing the amount of time you spend on A-column matters.

Of course, items will move across the grid as time passes. Tasks with deadlines will rise from the low-urgency level to the top of the grid. As events unfold some items may become more important – or less important – than at first they appeared. Note that some Low A's, however, will not naturally move up through the grid: these are important items, but they don't have deadlines – unless you give them one. They are things that are (or could be) very important to you, but no one else is pushing you to do them. They could include improving your skills or qualifications, arranging that holiday you've been promising yourself for some time, or making contact with people who could provide the advice, information and support you might need in the future. This is a good part of the grid to explore in more detail.

Prioritizing is by no means the complete solution to time management problems, but it is the best starting point.

REFERENCE
Covey, Stephen R., *The Seven Habits of Highly Effective People*, Simon & Schuster, 1992.

11. NLP

NLP (neuro-linguistic programming) is a model of models and processes aimed at the development of behaviours necessary for personal effectiveness and for effective interpersonal relationships. It brings together theories and practices based on how our brains work, the language we use to describe things and behavioural conditioning. There are perhaps four key models and three key processes:

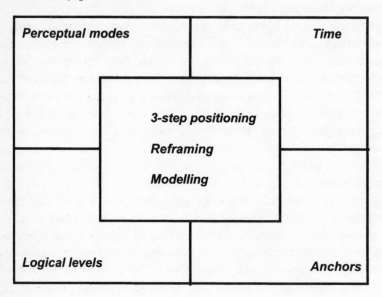

Key models
1. *Perceptual modes:* we each have a preference for receiving information visually (seeing), auditorially (hearing), or kin-aesthetically (touch and sensation). We can identify a person's preferences by: (a) their eye movements; and (b) the language they tend to use: e.g., 'The way I see it is . . .' or 'It sounds like you want . . .' If we understand other people's preferences, we can present information and ideas, and discuss them, in more appropriate ways.
2. *Time:* past, present and future. 'He is living in the past' is an example of when a problem of the present may actually be rooted in the past: a dispute between two people may not actually be about something in the here and now but more related to the there and then. We need to look at what time period we should be thinking and operating in.

3. *Logical levels:* there are five levels – identity, beliefs and values, capabilities, behaviour and environment. When addressing a people problem, we need to identify and address the root cause of the problem. For example, a person who makes a bad mistake at their job might lose their self-image of being a good worker; in effect they might lose some or all of their identity. If so, helping them to re-establish their identity through counselling or reassurance might be more important than addressing their capabilities, which is usually done through training.

4. *Anchors:* we all have past experiences we can recall, and in fact re-experience, in the here and now. We can relive the sensations we felt, we can re-think the thoughts. These experiences can be triggered accidentally by an external event – a song, a scent or taste, a photograph – or we can trigger them ourselves using positive anchors to evoke, for example, feelings of confidence, happiness or calm when we are under pressure.

Key processes

1. *3-step positioning:* this process is a way of becoming more objective, particularly when in actual or potential conflict with another person. First we examine things from our own viewpoint (first position), considering our own thoughts and feelings. Secondly we look at things from the other person's point of view (second position), trying to think and feel like them. Thirdly, we consider the two perspectives dispassionately from a detached viewpoint (third position).

2. *Reframing:* this is another process that aims to help us see, think and feel differently. A photographer uses his or her fingers to shape a rectangle to frame a possible picture. If we resize the frame, or angle it differently, we can see the same object in different ways, perhaps focusing in on specific parts. Reframing a problem means to see it in different ways, from different perspectives.

3. *Modelling:* many of our behaviours and ways of thinking and seeing are modelled on other people. From a very early age, we start to copy others. In NLP, we can use this natural tendency purposefully to learn expertise from those around us who are experts. We can copy them. Simply copying others is potentially dangerous, so NLP modelling requires us to identify not just what an expert might do but also what he

is thinking and feeling at the time. If we do this consciously, we can evaluate the pros and cons of not just doing as the expert does, but of thinking and feeling as the expert thinks and feels. We can get inside the expert's skin, but we can also choose the aspects that best suit us in our circumstances.

Using the models
Each one of the models in NLP could be treated as a separate model in this book. The four key models and three key processes are only sketched out here. There are other processes used such as developing sensory acuity, building rapport, mirroring, etc. NLP is in some ways a hotchpotch of ideas and methods that its practitioners are gradually pulling together to form a coherent and distinctive whole.

The best way of using the models is to become more familiar with them, sensitize yourself to them, and practise them. Much of NLP is to do with becoming more conscious of your own thoughts and feelings, and learning to manage them, enhancing the good points and replacing the less good with more appropriate ones.

REFERENCES
Beaver, Diana, *Lazy Learning*, Element, 1995.
O'Connor, Joseph, and Seymour, John, *An introduction to Neuro-linguistic programming*, Aquarius, 1993.

There are several practitioners' associations, for example:
Association for NLP, 48 Corser Street, Stourbridge West Midlands DY8 2DQ, Tel: 01384 443935.
The International Association of Master Trainers, The Brackens, London Road, Ascot, Berks. SL5 8BG, Tel: 01344 890263.

12. Thinking Hats

When we are faced with decisions or problems, our minds can be a muddle of thoughts. In decision-making meetings, the discussions may swing from positive to negative evaluations of a situation, and from rational analysis to highly emotional and intuitive assessments. Edward de Bono's six thinking hats can help us to be more aware of our instinctive patterns of thinking and to organize these thoughts and discussions in order to develop a richer understanding of events and issues.

De Bono's six hats represent the main patterns of thought, artificially separated. The value of the model lies in helping us to recognize which pattern of thought we are using (which hat we are wearing) when we react to a situation, and helping us to adopt a different pattern of thought (taking that hat off and trying on another).

The six hats are:

WHITE: neutral, objective thinking, concerned with facts
RED: emotional, intuitive thinking
BLACK: gloomy, negative, critical thinking
YELLOW: sunny, positive, optimistic thinking
GREEN: creative, innovative thinking
BLUE: cool, organized, summarizing thinking

The value of trying on other hats is perhaps greatest when we have looked at a situation for too long and have become negative about it (Black hat), or when we are becoming too emotional or relying too heavily on intuition (Red hat).

It is also useful, when we are facing complex situations that call for reactions of different kinds, to adopt the different patterns of thinking one at a time. White hat thinking is necessary to establish the known facts, for example, and Green hat thinking is useful for speculating on causes of problems, or possible solutions, while Blue hat thinking is needed for drawing together the contributions of different parties in a meeting.

Using the model
The thinking hats model can have a significant effect in helping you to achieve new viewpoints on situations and problems.

The hats can be successfully introduced to a team, and used to address management problems. They are less intrusive than some of the other models we have considered – such as assertiveness or TA – and easier to learn how to use quickly. As de Bono observes, the artificiality of the hats is a large part of their value.

The first stage in using the hats is to memorize their core meaning. The diagram below may help.

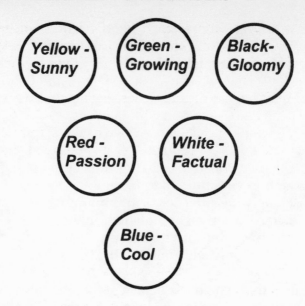

Typical questions for activating the different hats are:

WHITE: what are the facts?
RED: how do I feel about this? What is my gut feeling?
BLACK: what can go wrong?
YELLOW: how can I add these ideas together into a good plan?
          What are the benefits of doing this?
GREEN: is there a different way of looking at this? What new
          things could we do here?
BLUE: taking it all together, what should I do?

REFERENCE
de Bono, Edward, *Six Thinking Hats*, Penguin, 1987.

13. Creativity

Creative thinking is an important aspect of learning – because learning is an activity that often requires you to look at things in new ways. Creativity is also often a key element in successful decision-making – where you may need to think in new ways to identify the real issues, or to come up with good alternative courses of action. Some aspect of creative thinking is often identified as a key competency of effective managers, but creativity is frequently an area where some of our clients have a negative self-image: they initially see themselves as simply 'not creative'.

This self-image usually undergoes a change after we have introduced them to some techniques for thinking more innovatively. One of the best models we have found sets out the five phases of creative thought, first identified by David Campbell:

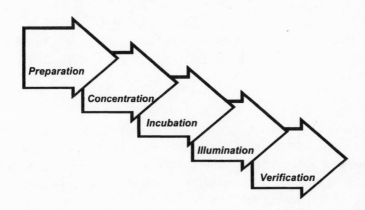

1. *Preparation:* we spend time studying the situation. We gather information and set about defining the problem.
2. *Concentration*: this preparation work intensifies, and – if it is an important issue – we may spend much time working on it, reframing the problem, looking at it from different viewpoints, identifying a range of possible answers and trying out some of the new solutions.
3. *Incubation:* we relax our direct focus on the problem, and spend some time away from the situation, usually thinking of something else. These may be short periods of time when we are driving home from the office, doing the washing-up, watching the television, taking the dog for a walk.
4. *Illumination:* during phase 3 our unconscious mind is still working on the problem, and insights and solutions arise. Phase 4 is what Campbell calls the 'Aha' moment – or what Archimedes called 'Eureka'.
5. *Verification:* we check the solution, and work out any practical problems.

This simple model places hard work squarely at the foundations of creativity, with preparation and concentration as the first two phases. Without the effort that is expended here, truly creative solutions are unlikely to be achieved.

The concentration phase can be wearying, however, and we can begin to feel very disheartened if we fail to produce a creative solution from the hard work. The model promotes the value of an incubation period, where a solution is more likely to arise if we relax our conscious focus on the problem and let our unconscious mind work on it.

Illumination is not guaranteed, of course – and sometimes the rays of light are from a false dawn, as our 'Aha' insight is simply a recollection of a solution we have already considered, evaluated and abandoned. Like all arts, creative thinking is unpredictable.

Using the model
The five phases of the model enable you to map out a rough schedule for developing new ideas – making sure enough time is allowed for each phase, whether you are working on something alone or organizing a group session.

The model indicates that you need to undertake intensive work to lay a foundation of understanding, to create familiarity with the facts, and to generate enough mental energy around the problem for it to be something that will incubate. You should then take a break away from this direct assault on the problem, but with the clear intent of making more progress after the break – and then make sure you review your decisions and ideas to take into account any creative insights that have developed.

REFERENCE
Campbell, David, *Take the road to creativity*, Center for Creative Leadership, Greensboro, S. Carolina, 1977.

14. Circles of Influence

A director once complained to us that his managers were coming up with solutions to problems they could do nothing about, yet couldn't find solutions to those they *could* do something about.

This simple model helps people to separate who and what they can influence from who and what they can't. Under pressure, in times of uncertainty, these may become confused.

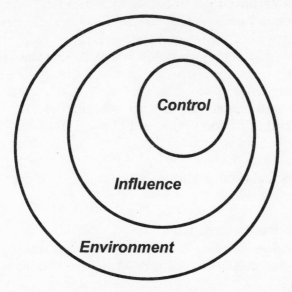

There are some issues that you and your team can control – these include problems you can solve with no outside assistance.

Then there are some issues over which you and your team have influence without complete control.

Finally there are some issues, problems or forces affecting you and the team that are part of the environment in which you operate. These are completely outside your control or influence.

Using the model
Use the diagram, or the idea of the three levels of influence, to categorize the problems and issues which affect you. Some issues will be easy to put into categories; in other cases it may be that you must test your assessment of your degree of influence and control in action. In reality, the distinction between categories may be a little blurred. It might be possible to influence one issue, for example, by going out of your way to gather support for your ideas – but you may still be unclear about how successful you are likely to be.

If you are considering the collective spheres of influence of your team, it is obviously helpful to discuss and use the model in team meetings, to raise awareness about the extent of your joint control and influence, and to focus attention in the first place on problems the team can do something about.

You can also use the model to consider how you can extend your sphere of influence.

Influence can be based on:

- position in the organization, which confers legitimate authority;
- purchasing power;
- expertise and knowledge in particular matters;
- track record of performance, and reputation;
- access to people with authority;
- alliances with others;
- good personal relationships;
- persuasive skills.

Can you identify areas where you would like to expand your sphere of influence? You might consider whether any of these components of influence can be used to help you do so.

REFERENCES
Covey, Stephen R., *The Seven Habits of Highly Effective People*, Simon & Schuster, 1992.

In a team context, or when dealing with operational problems, this model can be used alongside model 68.
For further aspects of power in organizations, see model 48.

SELF-DEVELOPMENT

A basic issue for people facing change and challenge is the extent to which they are able to learn and develop, and to acquire new skills. Are successful managers and leaders born, not made? Or can a person learn to lead? These questions quickly lead to attempts to describe what is natural and what is learned, and to understand and explain the processes of learning and development. A common, and not particularly helpful, mental model is that our abilities are relatively fixed. Skills – or the absence of them – are stable characteristics: 'I'm just disorganized'; 'You are a good negotiator'; 'He's good with computers'.

The work in this book is supported by our beliefs that:

1. We are all able to develop and change ourselves, our skills, our knowledge, our attitudes, our performance.
2. In a world of accelerating change, it is important to learn new skills, and to be adaptable to new circumstances.
3. Learning and development is not always easy or comfortable, and there are practical limits to how far we can change, and how long it will take us to do so, but we can all learn to do things tomorrow that we couldn't do yesterday.

In our efforts to change and develop, it is useful to understand some of the processes of learning. We have found the models on the following pages to be helpful in this respect.

15. Learning Needs Analysis

There are many tools available to help us assess learning needs, from simple self-analysis questionnaires through to sophisticated assessment centres. The tools tend to use models of good practice – of behaviours, competences or skills – against which we can measure ourselves and thus identify gaps and priorities.

Many diagnostic tools, especially questionnaires, are generic and can provide a general pointer to what is needed. It is usually better if individual needs analysis is carried out with a specific job or role and organization context in mind, since the required priorities and levels of abilities will differ from job to job. To be effective in a particular job in a particular organization, there is a need for congruence or fit between personal abilities, job demands and general organizational requirements.

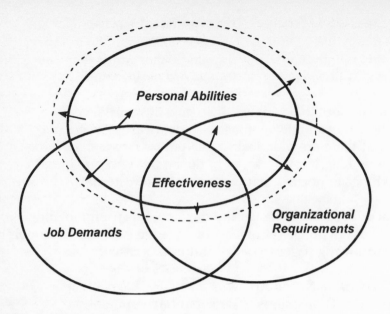

Based on Boyatzis, 1982

If effectiveness comes through matching our personal abilities to meet the demands of a particular job or role in the context of a particular organization, then the greater the overlap of the three circles, the more effective we will be.

Learning needs analysis should aim to identify which personal abilities we need to grow to be more effective in our job. We may also attempt to move the job to align it more with our abilities and interests. Senior managers could even be in a position to move or influence the organizational culture to align more with their abilities, and to make the organization in their image.

Using the model
If learning is to be relevant, then we need to think in terms of the specific skills and competences required by the job. You can think of the job as a whole and prepare a person specification (see model 36) for systematic comparison of your abilities. You can also be more focused. Any job task can be defined in terms of its component parts or in terms of the skills and competences required. For example, if your job involves leading meetings, then chairing a typical meeting might involve:

• getting the meeting going;
• guiding the meeting through the agenda;

- summarizing what has been agreed;
- seeing that written records are kept;
- managing conflicts and diversions;
- seeing that all participants have the opportunity to contribute, etc.

A list of personal skills and competences required might include:

- active listening;
- summarizing;
- conflict management;
- time management;
- mediation skills;
- making decisions;
- management of group problem-solving, etc.

Chairing meetings is just one example. Many of the other models in this book give indications of good practice in different areas. Depending on your job, and the area in which you are interested, you may have an organization-specific competence model to follow.

We work in the belief that any skill or behaviour can be learnt, in time, and it is helpful to have the well-defined starting point of a valid model or framework.

REFERENCE
Boyatzis, R. E., *The Competent Manager: A Model for Effective Performance*, Wiley, New York, 1982.

16. Three Dimensions of Personal Development

When we are asked to rate our ability in a skill or a competence, perhaps as a precursor to identifying particular learning needs, we are often given a rating scale. For example:

How effective are you at chairing a meeting?

| ------------- | ------------- | ------------- | ------------- | ------------- | ------------- |
 1   2   3   4   5   6   7

We may have difficulty giving a valid answer to this since 'effective' can be interpreted from a number of perspectives: there are three in particular – which can be described as quantity, range and quality.

Quantity – or consistency	How consistent are we at applying good practice at chairing meetings? We may be very skilful, but perhaps we do not always put the skill into practice.
Range	What type of meetings can we chair well? Can we identify the range of meetings in which we need to be effective? We may be able to chair more formal meetings, for example, where the procedures can help regulate the meetings, but we may be less able to chair informal meetings where more flexibility may be required – or vice versa.
Quality	One particular meeting may be easier to chair because everyone is working together well. At another meeting, with the same people, perhaps, the meeting may be significantly more difficult because two members have strongly conflicting views. Can we chair meetings where the quality of skills required is higher?

People using a single scale often tend to focus on quantity, with a particular instance or set of instances in mind. Afterwards they may say, 'I scored myself this way, but I could have scored myself differently if I had focused on a different set of circumstances.'

The three dimensions are related, so we may need to take an iterative approach to assessing ourselves. For example, each time we identify a new aspect of range (a different set of circumstances we need to tackle), we may need to consider quality and quantity for those circumstances.

Low self-assessment scores in quality and range indicate that there are skills and knowledge we need to develop. Learning may be of higher-level skills, or it may involve exposure to a wider set of experiences, or both.

Low assessments in quantity may indicate that we have the knowledge and skills to be effective, but that something is preventing us from applying them. This may be a motivational issue, or a need to practise the skill to a greater degree and achieve unconscious competence.

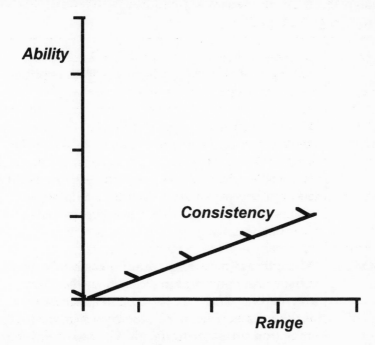

If we are now asked the same rating question, perhaps we could plot ourselves in the three dimensions.

Using the model
You can use the model to make the diagnosis of your development needs more specific, so that you can target the right development focus.

Select a best-practice model of skills or behaviour in the area you wish to consider, and separately rate yourself in each dimension. If there are significant differences in the range of circumstances in which you are acting – or expect to act – it may be most effective to identify these first, and concentrate on one set of circumstances – those which are most important to you – assessing yourself for quality and consistency in each area of the range.

For quality and range shortfalls, attempt to identify the specific skills and areas of experience you need in order to improve your performance. Beware of using 'Quality' as a label that obscures what these specific skills might be.

For consistency shortfalls, consider why you fall short of what is required. Time pressure perhaps? Laziness or forgetfulness? How can you overcome these problems and become more consistent?

REFERENCE
Boak, G., 'Three Dimensions of Personal Development', *Industrial and Commercial Training*, Vol. 23, No. 5, 1991.

17. Learning Cycle

The learning cycle is a model of how people develop skills. It explains the different types of activity we need to undertake in order to be effective learners. There are two widely used versions of this model: the American version, designed by David Kolb; and the British version, developed by Peter Honey and Alan Mumford. In the Honey and Mumford model the four learning activities are: undertaking *Action*; *Reflecting* on performance; developing *Theories* to explain performance, or researching the theories and ideas of others; and *Planning* the next occasion of action. In order to develop any skill, a learner must undertake each of these activities, perhaps on several occasions.

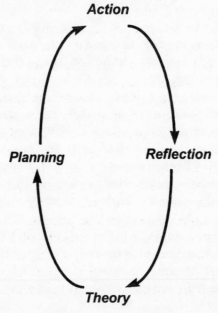

Action

Planning   **Reflection**

Theory

Suppose you make a presentation to a group of senior managers – the action stage of the cycle. Perhaps it is not as well received as you would have liked. You reflect on what you did – which parts seemed to work well, which were less effective? You may seek feedback from others to help you in this stage of the cycle. Eventually you reach some conclusions – the theory stage – about how to give successful presentations to this group. You may have been helped by some theory from elsewhere – by reading books on the subject, or attending courses, or listening to advice from others. Your theory may be an elaborate set of principles, or it may be a short checklist of key points. Finally, as a new opportunity arises, you undertake some planning about how to tackle the next presentation. This new action stage is also followed by reflection, and perhaps some additions or amendments to the theory, and there will be more planning before the next presentation, and so on. It may take many trips around the cycle before you are as proficient as you would like to be.

Using the model
This is a simple, durable and very effective model for thinking about the learning process, which can provide a sturdy framework for planning skills development, particularly if it is used in conjunction with the learning styles model on the following pages.

Use the model to structure your action plan for developing a skill: are all four activities represented in your plan? You can't, for example, expect to learn new skills simply by reading about them, or by observing other people performing them: you need to undertake the action phase yourself. On the other hand, you are unlikely to develop skills purely by action, either. Some reflection and evaluation (perhaps with the help of feedback and advice from others) will be necessary, too.

Use the model for evaluating your learning. This can be especially valuable in areas where you are having problems – if you are learning how to work with a difficult individual, for example, or an aggressive group of people. It can help to keep a learning journal, containing accounts of key events: What happened? (Action.) What is your assessment of how you – and they – behaved? (Reflection.) What conclusions can you draw from this? Does it fit with any recognized framework – such as the ideas on assertiveness? (Theory.) What would you do differently next time? What will you do next? (Planning.)

REFERENCE
Honey, Peter, and Mumford, Alan, *The Manual of Learning Styles*, Peter Honey, Maidenhead, 1988.

18. Learning Styles

The learning cycle on the previous pages identifies four types of activity that people must undertake in order to develop skills: planning, acting, reflecting and theorizing.

Peter Honey and Alan Mumford believe that each of us has different preferences for these four stages of the cycle, and they have developed a self-analysis questionnaire to identify these preferences, or learning styles.

The result is a score between 1 and 20 for each of the four learning activities.

An individual's learning styles profile may show a high score for one or two of the learning activities – indicating the general shape of an ideal approach for that particular individual to learning new skills. High activists, for example, will prefer to begin with involvement and learning-by-doing, whereas high theorists are likely to prefer to learn the rules and principles of the new skill area.

The profile may also show significantly low scores for one or more of the learning activities. Low activists, for example, may shrink away from trying to put the skill into practice. Low theorists may have difficulty in reaching conclusions on principles (and may avoid reading or otherwise learning the principles other people have reached) about the skill area. These omissions can seriously hinder a person's ability to learn new skills.

The Learning Styles Questionnaire (LSQ) is not purely about our approach to learning, however, but more about our attitudes to life experiences, and it can cast a quick bright light on some of our patterns of behaviour.

In brief:

- *Activists:* high activists enjoy new experiences, excitement and drama, high visibility and being thrown in at the deep end; low activists may plan and theorize and review events, but their level of spontaneous, unplanned activity is much lower.
- *Reflectors:* high reflectors enjoy being able to stand back and listen and observe, thinking before acting, reviewing and analysing events; low reflectors tend not to observe and evaluate events to such an extent, and therefore often fail to build on successes and are prone to repeat failures.
- *Theorists:* high theorists enjoy exploring ideas and concepts, relating specific events to general theories; low theorists have difficulty in reaching summaries and conclusions, and in gaining value from principles and abstractions, and therefore often fail to understand the similarities and differences between situations.
- *Pragmatists:* high pragmatists enjoy learning about techniques with a practical use, learning from role models, putting techniques into practice; low pragmatists tend to arrive in situations unprepared, having failed to think ahead about what might be required.

Common profiles are of high pragmatist-activist and high reflector-theorist.

Although the accuracy of self-assessment exercises is always open to question, we have had good results with the LSQ. Clients of all ages and backgrounds have been interested in the results, and some of their profiles have been very clearly validated by their actions in the workplace.

Using the model
A working understanding of learning styles is helpful when planning any kind of learning or training.

An understanding of your own style preferences can help you to choose methods that you will most enjoy – but it will also alert you to areas where there may be weaknesses, and the learning process may suffer if you do not take special care. This may mean taking more formal measures to ensure that you carry out the activities which are low preference for you: targeting a number of activities you will carry out (for a low activist); keeping a learning journal and targeting a minimum number of entries each week (for a low reflector); targeting a minimum amount of time to be spent on reading new ideas (for a low theorist); or setting out a clear plan in a certain format (for a low pragmatist).

When working with other people, it is useful to be aware of differences in styles: for example, a difference between the preferred style of a coach and that of a learner may mean that exercises are chosen which will not especially suit the latter.

REFERENCES
The Learning Styles Questionnaire is published by Peter Honey.
Honey, Peter, and Mumford, Alan, *The Manual of Learning Styles*, Peter Honey, Maidenhead, 1988.

19. *Motivation to Learn*

The many books on learning and self-development often seem to convey the message that success in these activities is simply a matter of knowing and applying the right techniques: that these are essentially straightforward matters, which can be achieved through rational planning, a little self-discipline and a little effort. In fact, in our experience, the business of learning and self-development is often more difficult than this, and in addition to the rational planning, self-discipline and effort, there are usually emotional and motivational factors to take into account.

At times these are positive: the exhilaration of early successes fuels the desire to spend more time learning – doing more reading, or more practice. At other times the dominant emotion is frustration or annoyance, and motivation is at a low ebb.

We have developed a model of the main factors that appear to affect the motivation to learn – which are particularly appropriate for attempts to acquire skills. The model can be useful when you are attempting to train or coach another person, but it is also relevant for those times when you yourself are trying to learn a new skill.

People will only learn when:

1. They accept they have a *need* to learn. In the context of work-related skills this usually means an acceptance that they have a performance problem, or a skills gap.

2. They believe that they have the potential *ability* to learn the
   required skill. Some people may accept that they have a need
   – they are unable to do something – but doubt whether they
   can improve on their present performance. Many (older)
   people in recent years have stumbled at this stage over
   learning IT skills.
3. They believe that learning this skill is a *priority*. Some people
   can accept points 1 and 2 – that they have a need and the
   potential ability to learn the skill – but they then consider all
   the other demands on their time and allocate the necessary
   learning a low priority.

If any one of these three beliefs is not present, people are
unlikely to learn.

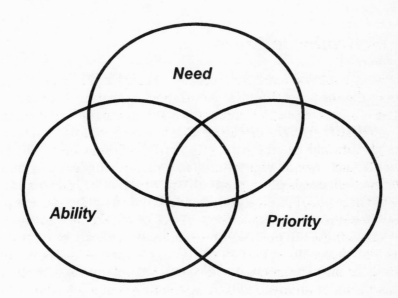

Using the model
This model of need, ability and priority makes a valuable,
simple checklist when trying to train or coach someone else. Is
there a blockage at any of the three points that needs to be
addressed? Can you make progress on clearing the blockage by
challenging it, or discussing it? If you are unable to make
progress in clearing the blockage, then any time spent on
training is likely to be wasted.

As a checklist for your own learning, the model can also be
helpful. At the outset, as you contemplate learning how to do

something new, or improving on a skill you already possess to some degree, it is worth checking your beliefs at each of the three points in the model. Is this really a need? Do you believe you are able to learn what is required? Is it a priority?

As and when difficulties arise, or when the learning curve reaches a plateau, it is useful to check again on each of the three points. Has your inner dialogue become negative and doubtful? Is there a good reason for this?

The results of this self-enquiry may lead you to the conclusion that the situation has indeed changed, and there is no longer a need to develop this skill, or this is no longer a priority for you, or your ability to learn the skill is indeed very limited. But it may be that the enquiry confirms your original (but now wavering) beliefs, and you continue your efforts with renewed motivation.

REFERENCE
See also model 22; and the section on inner dialogue in model 2.

20. Double Loop Learning

When we encounter a new problem, we may analyse it, determine its causes, develop alternative solutions, select one and implement it. If we are correct in our analysis, the problem will be solved.

For example, suppose someone calls me to say they can no longer keep an appointment we had arranged for next week. Something else has come up. We look through our diaries and arrange another appointment.

Another example: suppose my new supplies of headed paper have just been returned from the printing company. I notice that the printing is not of a good standard: the colours overlap on many of the sheets. I telephone the printer and complain, and he agrees to reprint the order.

In each case I have undertaken a series of activities which can best be represented as a single loop: I have solved these two problems – on one level.

In each case I might have questioned some of my underlying assumptions in approaching the problem. This might lead to a reframing or redefinition of the problem.

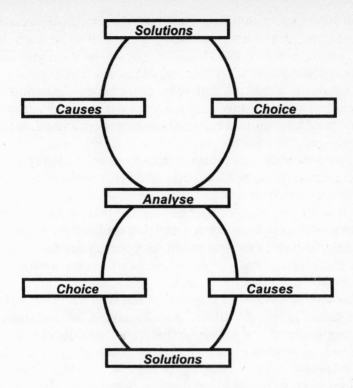

In the first example, I might question whether the appointment is really necessary or of value: instead of meeting, can we discuss the matter over the phone? Or is there someone else that I could meet about this matter? Is there someone else the other person could meet? Or instead of a short weekday meeting, should we have a social visit over a weekend? If this re-arrangement, instigated by the other person, is a regular occurrence, I might wonder whether I should re-evaluate our longer-term working relationship.

In the second example, I might re-evaluate how I have specified my requirements to the printer in the past – perhaps the problem could have been avoided if I had been clear about what I wanted? I might redesign the headed paper to omit the colours. I might consider taking my business to a new printing company.

In each case, not only do I go through the same activities as before – analysing causes, considering solutions, etc. – but I also review the broader factors surrounding the immediate problem.

This can be represented as a double loop: the immediate

problem is tackled, but any broader problem is also considered – and if necessary also tackled.

Using the model
The model is a simple but effective reminder to think about broader and/or longer-term implications of immediate problems. Obviously, it is not always appropriate to take action at this higher level. In our examples, the rearranged appointment may be a solution that is entirely adequate and the printing error may be a one-off occurrence, which is promptly rectified.

It can be useful to practise with this model, however, particularly to apply it to any recurring problems you encounter. As a practice exercise, you might set yourself the discipline of at least considering how you could go about double-loop analyzing three problems a day for a week.

This model has been extended to the way in which problems are tackled in organizations, too. In single-loop learning, the problem is addressed purely at the operational level, whereas in double-loop learning there is a reconsideration of policy and more strategic goals.

The implication of this is that there must be a flow of information – about any operational issues that should be considered in the second loop – to those who make the policy. Do these flows exist inside your organization? Do they operate effectively? How could they be improved?

References
'Double loop learning' is an expression first used by Chris Argyris and Donald Schon. See: Argyris, C., and Schon, D., *Organizational Learning: A theory of action perspective*, Addison Wesley, 1978.
Pedler, M., Burgoyne, J., and Boydell, T., *The Learning Company*, McGraw Hill, 1991.

See also model 58.

21. Developing Competence

There are a number of recognizable stages in learning a skill.

The first stage is a state of unconscious incompetence: we are so unaware of the skill area, we do not realize that we are incompetent. Imagine someone chairing a meeting who has no knowledge of the principles and rules they should apply, and who has not observed a good role model.

The second stage is a rise to a state of conscious incompetence. Our performance may be no better than it was before, but at least we are aware of our shortcomings. Imagine our chair of meetings in the early stages of a short course to develop this skill area: there is as yet no improvement in ability, but at least they now know he should be behaving differently.

With practice, with the acquisition of new skills and knowledge, our performance improves to the point where we might say we have become competent – but we are conscious of what we are doing to be effective. At this stage we may be a little awkward or mechanical about some of the things we do.

With more practice, much of what we have been doing is internalized and becomes second nature, to the extent that we do it unconsciously.

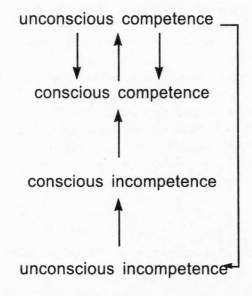

unconscious competence

conscious competence

conscious incompetence

unconscious incompetence

At this stage we need to be careful that unconscious competence doesn't drift back into unconscious *incompetence* – through carelessness, overconfidence, or some significant changes in the situation. In key skill areas it can be helpful to remind ourselves from time to time of the principles of good practice, and to seek feedback on our performance – in other words, to move back deliberately into the conscious competence stage from time to time.

Using the model

As consultants and trainers we have found this to be a very valuable model for people who are trying to understand the nature and extent of their development as they work to improve their skills. As with all models, it simplifies reality: in practice there are degrees of competence, and a learner does not suddenly step across a line from incompetence one day to competence the next. In the same way, there are degrees of consciousness through which we move, rather than the two neat categories of the model.

However, the model can be an excellent aid in developing your skills (and, of course, developing the skills of members of your team).

Useful activities at each stage are:

Unconscious incompetence	Gather feedback on performance Read about good practice Observe good role models Identify areas of incompetence
Conscious incompetence	Continue with the above and . . . Learn to recognize competent performance Identify the key target areas for your learning and make learning plans Practise, and review progress – using the learning cycle model
Conscious competence	Continue with the learning cycle activities Continue to gather feedback Practise, practise, practise
Unconscious competence	Occasionally reflect on and review performance Occasionally gather feedback, especially on key skill areas for your job Occasionally refresh yourself with ideas about good practice

22. Learning Curve

The learning curve is a pattern that can be plotted when we are learning a skill where our performance can be measured – such as many production and construction tasks. It can also be experienced – if not measured – in other skill development areas.

At the beginning, if learning is successful, there may be rapid improvements in performance over a short period of time (at part A of the curve in the diagram below) which then level out into a plateau (at points B and C). As different parts of the skill are assimilated, performance may improve again (at point D) before again flattening out into a plateau.

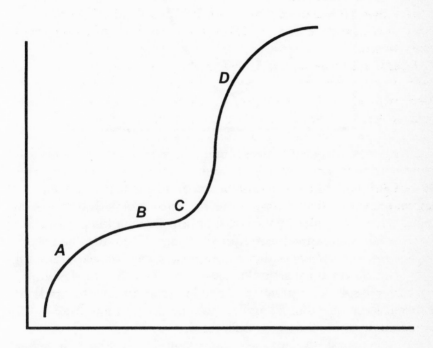

Learning curve showing improvements in performance over time

Using the Model
Understanding the nature of the learning curve is important for individual learners, for trainers and for managers. The obvious message is that the pace of improvement in a skill or a knowledge area is not constant, but will at times be rapid and dramatic and at other times negligible. The shape of our example above is not necessarily the shape of every learning curve: in fact, the early stages of approaching a new area of knowledge and skill may show very little improvement in performance. Where we attempt to change the way we do

something, by learning a different approach, our performance may at first get worse – and follow the shape of the J curve, below.

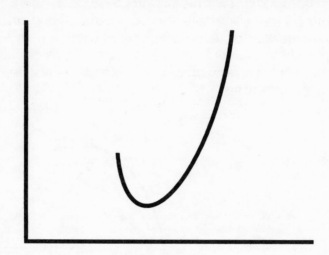

At times of rapid improvement, the motivation to learn is usually high, because we are seeing immediate results. When improvement tapers off, however, and reaches a plateau – or when performance follows the first dip of the J curve – our motivation may dwindle. If further improvement is possible it is important to maintain our efforts to learn. There may be reasons for, and ways beyond, the plateau we are experiencing, depending on the particular skill we are trying to develop. It may be that further practice is needed to assimilate the skill at a level of unconscious competence – or it may be that a slightly different approach is now called for.

Keyboard skills are a good example of an area where performance is measurable. The first plateau is reached when we are able to find all the letters easily and quickly on the keyboard. Progress is made beyond this when instead of typing individual letters, we are able to type words; progress beyond the second plateau is achieved when we begin to recognize and type in the patterns of phrases.

The learning curve can also have an impact on company strategy, because it can have important implications for a company's costs. A company that moves into a new market, and has its production staff move up the learning curve ahead of its competitors, will be more productive, and can compete more effectively on price.

23. Information for Learning

In order to develop, especially if we are to develop in a planned way, we need to gather information about ourselves, how well we perform and how others see us. This model identifies the many sources of information available to us.

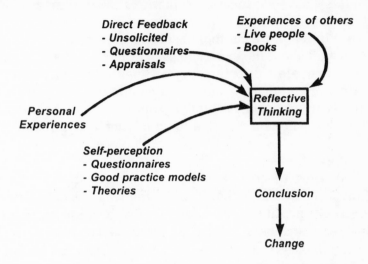

Personal experiences

This means identifying and learning from both mistakes and successes. If you are a good observer of events, and a good observer of yourself in those events, you should be able to identify what you did, said, thought and felt. You may also be able to identify the same for anyone else who might have been involved in the event. By reflecting honestly on these observations, without filtering out those things you do not wish to see, you should be able to identify what to do, say, think and feel differently in the future. Do you keep a log of your experiences? Do you try out new experiences in order to learn new things about yourself?

Self-perception

We each have a self-image that has been built up over the years. In order to learn and develop, it is helpful to test this, preferably in structured ways. We can use questionnaires or compare ourselves against models of good practice, or against theories of how to behave. Questionnaires such as the Myers-Briggs and the 16PF (see model 6) are statistically sound, and are constructed so as to be reliable and valid. Other questionnaires, even simple ones, can be useful if they stimulate you to look at yourself in a structured way.

Experiences of others

We learned in childhood to copy the behaviours of certain other people. It is a natural process that many of us continue to use as adults. If we use this natural process in a more managed way, we can turn it into a powerful tool of self-development.

We can read about the experiences of others, and/or we can go and ask people directly. Sometimes we might seek straightforward advice ('What would you do in this situation?'); sometimes we might ask for accounts of other people's experiences ('When he said that to you, what did you reply?').

Direct feedback

Sometimes we get feedback without asking. An angry customer might make a complaint about something we have done wrong, a pleased boss might say, 'Well done.' If we want to make more use of direct feedback, it is best to go and ask for it.

Conclusions and change

After gathering this information, we need to draw some conclusions. Self-discovery tends to be an ongoing process, but it is usually valuable to write your conclusions down, as you find them at the time. This helps to crystallize your thinking, and provides a solid foundation for a personal change plan.

Using the model

The model emphasizes the range of sources of information that you can use to establish your strengths and your development needs. It is natural to have preferences for some of these sources over others – but this shouldn't lead you to ignore some sources altogether.

Soliciting direct feedback from others is often particularly valuable. It is helpful to structure the questions you ask – perhaps using one or more of the good practice models in this book as a framework, and creating a rating scale – in order to help people to give you information that is clear and specific enough for you to act on it.

Leading and Managing

In this section of the book we include models specifically related to leading, managing and supervising the activities of other people.

There are many simple images of the relationships between managers and the people they attempt to lead: shepherd and sheep, parent and child, military metaphors favouring clear instructions and firm decisions from commanding officers, sporting analogies featuring team captains. These images may indeed on occasion appear to capture the roles that are played – albeit only for brief moments before the participants move on and another, more complex model appears more appropriate.

Management is famously an activity which produces results only through the work of other people, and therefore there is a high premium on understanding others and being able to work well with them.

Beliefs which support the models in this section are:

1. On the whole, working co-operatively with others is preferable to being in conflict or in competition with them.
2. It is useful to attempt to understand other people, and to be aware of the possible problems, misunderstandings and barriers to communication and co-operation that can arise in our relationships with them.
3. The effectiveness of most managers and professionals depends very much on how well they work with other people.

A number of the models in the previous section are, of course, of value in this area. The assertiveness models, Parent, Adult, Child and Life Positions are of particular value in helping us to manage our relationships with others. The personal effectiveness models – particularly SMART, Time Management and Circles of Influence – are of as much relevance to managing the work of a team as they are to self-management. The models on learning and self-development can be applied by managers in their role of coach and mentor to help understand and facilitate the development of others.

In this section there are models on the nature of management and leadership – where opinions and trends have been changing in recent years, moving towards styles of greater empowerment, requiring greater commitment from others.

We include a number of middle range models on motivation. Each individual we manage may want different things, but there are patterns in the ways people evidence and pursue their needs and wants. There are also useful models on team working, which can be of value to team leaders and members alike.

As well as leading the team in order to produce results today, managers are also charged with developing team members in order to produce better – or different – results tomorrow. There are a small number of models on aspects of training and development, which should be used in conjunction with the models on self-development in the previous section. Finally, there is a model specifically about managing problem people – although many of the more general models can be used in this context, too.

Models in other sections of the book are also relevant to the role of team leader. In Achieving Results there are a number of frameworks that are useful for addressing the practical problems and decisions that can face a team; and in Change there are perspectives on persuasion and influence that managers increasingly need in order to win the commitment of the people with whom they work.

24. Leaders and Managers
25. Action-Centred Leadership
26. Leadership Styles
27. The Functions of Management
28. The Outputs of Management
29. Motivation – the Process
30. What Motivates People?
31. Theory X and Theory Y
32. Team Working
33. Team Roles
34. Flexible and Self-Managed Teams
35. Team Briefing
36. Person Specification
37. Skills Grids
38. The Training Triangle
39. Coaching
40. Modifying Behaviour

24. Leaders and Managers

In recent years we have seen a significant change in models of leadership and management.

For many years, the dominant view was that the exercise of leadership was part of a manager's job: leadership related in particular to the manager leading the immediate team, and involved motivating them, and directing and reviewing their actions.

Zaleznik introduced a different model, based around change, where management is about implementation and maintaining current operations, while leadership is about setting new directions and initiating changes.

Following Zaleznik, Bennis and Nanus defined the activity of management as 'to bring about, to accomplish, to have charge of or responsibility for, to conduct'. Whereas leadership is 'influencing, guiding in direction, course, action, opinion'. They summarized their position as: 'Managers are people who do things right and leaders are people who do the right things.'

Bennis and Nanus pictured a key part of the role of an effective leader as:

- establishing a vision of a clear and compelling goal;
- communicating the vision effectively to others, to win their support and co-operation.

In a similar vein John Kotter saw leadership as:

- establishing direction: developing a vision of the future and strategies for producing the changes needed to achieve the vision;
- aligning people: communicating the vision to all those whose co-operation may be needed, and influencing the creation of teams and coalitions that will support the vision;
- motivating and inspiring: energizing people to overcome major barriers to change.

Management was represented in Kotter's model by the traditional and rational activities of planning, budgeting, organizing and staffing, controlling and problem-solving.

This model of leadership is partly built on James MacGregor Burns' ideas of a transformational leader. According to Burns:

- transformational leadership inspires others to a 'continuing pursuit of a higher purpose', raising both leaders and followers 'to higher levels of motivation and morality', and is partly charismatic; whereas . . .
- transactional leadership is simply based on rational authority (or economic power): people obey such leadership because it is their job to do so, and they are rewarded by employment, pay, advancement, commendation, or shares of the spoils.

Closely linked to the enthusiasm for inspirational leadership are some views about the importance of managers being able to influence people over whom they have no authority.

It is arguable that in order to create a new perspective on leadership these writers exaggerated their case by demoting management to the status of proceduralized administration, but they did successfully identify a series of activities – centred around influencing and motivating others – that seem to be vitally important in effective performance and, in particular, in bringing about change within and across organizations. Some organizations have interpreted the message in pragmatic ways – they value both the management skills and the skills of leadership – and in profiling their employees they aim to develop people who are high in both sets of skills.

Leadership

High leadership low management	High leadership high management
Low leadership low management	Low leadership high management

Management

Using the models
The models provide a valuable challenge to some of our unconscious ideas of leadership and management, which emphasize the formal authority of the leader/manager, rather than the ability to influence and inspire. The models also promote the importance of change in successful organizations – and they complement other models you will find later in the book, in the section on Change.

A word of warning: in our experience, as you use the models, you should beware of slipping too enthusiastically to the extremes of transformational leadership. In particular, the word 'vision' is currently overused in management circles. If you can describe a clear and desirable state of affairs, towards which you would like everyone to work, then go ahead and describe it, as persuasively as possible, but leave the word 'vision' out of your script.

REFERENCES
Bennis, W., and Nanus, B., *Leaders: the Strategies for Taking Charge*, Harper Business, 1997 (2nd edn).
Burns, James MacGregor, *Leadership*, Harper and Row, 1978.
Kotter, J., *A Force for Change*, The Free Press, 1990.
Zaleznik, A., 'Managers and Leaders: Are They Different?', *Harvard Business Review*, May/June 1977, pp 67–78.

25. *Action-Centred Leadership*

One of the most popular models of a manager's role as a leader of a team is the action-centred leadership model of John Adair.

According to Adair, effective team leaders will pay attention to three main factors: the task, or what is to be achieved; the goals and development needs of the team; and the goals and development needs of individual team members.

Successful leadership is represented by the point where the three circles overlap. Unbalanced (and therefore unsuccessful) leadership is represented by an overlap of only two circles – for example, the leader operating on the overlap between Individual and Task is neglecting the development needs of the team as a whole. Very unbalanced leadership is represented by a concentration on only one of the three factors.

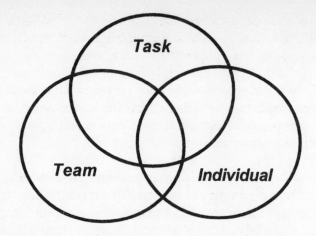

Actions that the successful manager will undertake include:

- *the task:* goal-setting, planning, allocating work and resources, monitoring and controlling progress;
- *the team:* taking steps to ensure integration of effort, encouraging co-operation between team members, developing team spirit, and resolving conflicts;
- *the individual:* delegation to particular projects, training, coaching, counselling, appraisal and giving individual feedback.

The model has been taken as the framework for a number of successful corporate programmes, where it supports training activities to produce balanced leadership – and to develop the range of skills which are required in order to carry out the necessary action in all three key areas.

The simplicity of the basic model is a part of its strength, but also the three functions are sufficiently different in nature for individual managers to exhibit significant strengths in one area, and significant weaknesses in the others – or for managers to neglect one area for too long while they concentrate on another.

Using the model
Use the model as a framework for a review of your activities in relation to your team.

- What task-orientated, goal-achieving activities do you carry out? How effective/successful are you in relation to these activities?

- What team-related activities do you carry out? What steps do you take to integrate and co-ordinate activities and to encourage good team spirit? How important is this in your job?
- What do you do about the needs of individual members of your team? What development, training, coaching, counselling do you undertake? What feedback and support do you provide? How important is this in your job?

It is possible for team leaders to achieve good results in the short term by focusing most of their efforts on achieving task results, and neglecting to a great extent the team and individual elements, but Adair's model indicates that this will lead to failure in the longer term. The frequent excuse of such managers – that there simply isn't time to focus on individual and team development and still achieve the desired task results – is also valid only in the short term, if at all. In the longer term, time spent on developing the team and the individual members of staff should repay the investment by increasing the capability of the team to achieve results.

If your self-assessment indicates to you that you are neglecting one or more areas of the leader role, make a realistic plan to restore the balance over a period of time. Small, frequent activities are more likely to make a positive difference than a sudden, unsustained spate of energetic team-building, or individual development activities, or a new enthusiasm for clear action plans and reformed monitoring systems.

REFERENCES
Adair, John, *Action Centred Leadership*, Gower, 1979.

See also models 8, 32 and 39.

26. Leadership Styles

For many years there has been an interest in the most effective way of managing the relationship between the leader of a team and its other members. An early model of two contrasting leadership styles was that of the autocratic leader and the democratic leader – and this simple model still sticks in the mind of many practising managers who have not thought more deeply about the matter. A development of this approach was to flesh out the continuum between autocratic and democratic leadership behaviour.

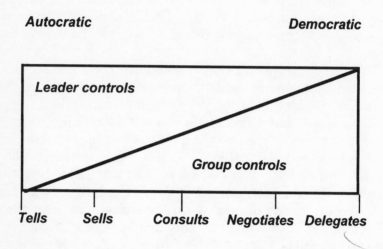

Leadership Styles
Based on Tannenbaum and Schmidt, 1973.

For Tannenbaum and Schmidt, effective leadership entails flexibility about style – and an effective leader will use a style that is appropriate to the situation. Their model identified factors that should indicate the most effective style, including:

- factors to do with the team members, such as maturity, skill, interest and motivation;
- factors to do with the situation, such as the nature of the problem, the degree of time pressure, the type of organization.

A second approach to leadership styles is the situational leadership model, produced by Hersey and Blanchard. They consider that a manager's role is to develop team members by building their skills, commitment and confidence, and by using the appropriate leadership style.

Their four leadership styles are combinations of task-orientated (or directive) behaviour and relationship-orientated (or supportive) behaviour.

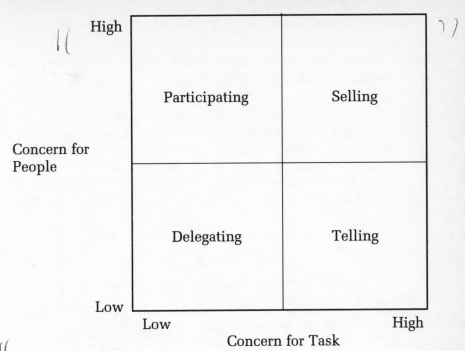

Situational Leadership
Based on Hersey and Blanchard, 1993.

Telling – providing specific instructions and closely supervising performance – is most appropriate when the team member is low in skill and also low in motivation or self-confidence.

Selling – explaining and discussing decisions the manager has made – is most appropriate when the team member is low in skills, but is motivated and interested.

Participating – sharing ideas and supporting the team member in making decisions – is appropriate when the team member is skilled, but is not entirely confident or motivated.

Delegating – giving responsibility for decisions to the team member – is appropriate when the team member is both willing and capable.

Using the models
The Hersey and Blanchard model is probably one of the most popular style models with practising managers and with management developers and trainers. Its basic premise is simple, but the authors have developed it for a variety of uses.

The value of both these models lies first in providing a more subtle view of the range of appropriate leadership styles than the simple autocrat/democrat divide of popular imagination. On the autocrat/democrat divide, practically every manager we have encountered would profess to be a democrat – although their behaviour often indicated differently. Both of these models give a range of styles, and also indicate factors that might reasonably lead us to adopt one style over another.

A simple use of either model is as a framework for auditing your own preferred style(s) of leadership. Do you have a preference for one or more styles? Do you have higher skills in some style areas? Do you have development needs in other areas?

REFERENCES

Hersey, R., and Blanchard, K. H., *Management of Organizational Behaviour*, Prentice Hall, 1993 (6th edn).

Tannenbaum, R., and Schmidt, W. H., 'How to Choose a Leadership Pattern', *Harvard Business Review*, May/June 1973.

27. The Functions of Management

A model of the functions of management is often used as an introduction to the area for students and novices, to whom it presents an overall map of the whole territory. One of the earliest tracts on management from the beginning of this century, by the industrialist Henri Fayol, followed this approach and defined the functions of management as: forecasting, planning, organizing, staffing, directing, co-ordinating, controlling, reviewing and budgeting. Fayol then proceeded to provide advice on what was required for good performance of each of these functions.

To a large extent the functions identified by Fayol are still alive today, although the list is usually shortened, with some of his functions absorbed by others. A cycle we have found useful is planning, organizing, motivating, co-ordinating and controlling (based on Koontz) – which can be used for small projects or large-scale operations:

- *planning* includes gathering information, forecasting future events, setting goals and objectives, establishing action plans;

- *organizing* includes gathering the necessary resources, including people, and delegating the authority and responsibility for carrying out the components of the action plan;
- *motivating* includes providing leadership and direction (which may be through a participative or directive leadership style) and encouraging people to achieve the goals;
- *co-ordinating* includes ensuring that the separate tasks, and the efforts of different individuals, combine together to achieve the overall goal;
- *controlling* includes checking on progress and taking the necessary action when events drift from the target levels.

These functions can be seen as two cycles, with motivating happening throughout. Planning and controlling feed into one another as the dominant management cycle, and organizing (which separates and distributes) is complemented by co-ordinating (which brings back together and combines).

This is a traditional model of management, and it has been criticized as unrealistic by, among others, Henry Mintzberg. In reality, individual managers will indeed rarely follow the implied stately progression from planning through organizing to motivating and so on: the categories overlap to a considerable extent. Despite its limitations, we have found this model of functions useful, however, as a framework for analysing the management of a project or a process, or as a checklist for planning purposes.

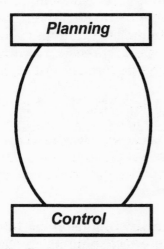

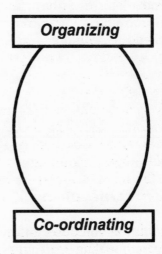

Using the model

Consider a project or an operation carried out by your organization, or by your department or team – ideally an operation or project where the expected results have not been achieved. The operation could be the provision of a single product or service, (or of a number of goods and services) to a particular market.

Note how each of the functions is carried out in relation to the project or operation:

How are activities planned? How is control carried out? (See models 64 and 67.)

How are resources gathered and organized? How is co-ordination achieved within the project or operation? How is the project or operation co-ordinated with other related activities? (See model 32.)

How are people motivated? (See the models 30 and 31.)

Are there problems at any of these stages? How can they be resolved?

This exercise may show that there is a basic flaw in the management of the project or activity – for example a lack of co-ordinating mechanisms, or an absence of control measures. The analysis may identify a problem which lies across a number of the functions – for example, the failure of a project co-ordinating committee to work effectively, partly because of the different motivations of its members, resulting in poor control and delayed planning – but the examination of the situation on a function-by-function basis can be helpful in identifying the effects of the problem, and perhaps pointing to solutions.

REFERENCES
Fayol, Henri, *General and Industrial Management*, Pitman, 1949.
Koontz, H., and Weihrich, H., *Management*, McGraw Hill, 1988 (9th edn).
Kotter, J., *A Force for Change*, The Free Press, 1990.
Mintzberg, H., *The Nature of Managerial Work*, Harper and Row, 1973.

28. The Outputs of Management

Conventional job descriptions often emphasize the discharge of duties rather than the achievement of results; activities rather than outcomes. They use words such as *maintain, plan, organize, lead, liaise* and *schedule.*

However the effect of management activity should be the achievement of certain results. Just as organizations can be seen as systems, with inputs, processing activities and outputs, so can the activities of a manager.

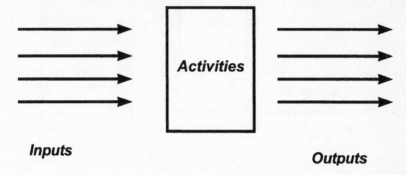

Inputs

Outputs

So the manager's task can be described in terms of outputs he or she will produce. Activity descriptions are thus translated into specifications of outputs, for example:

Maintain machines (activity) ———→ Machine availability at x% (output)

Planning (activity) ———→ Clear, written plans at a specified time (output)

Because managers achieve results through working with other people, there are issues of causality in relation to some outputs. The organization needs to achieve business results – sales, profits, productivity and successful outcomes to various projects. Individual managers may contribute to these organizational goals, but the extent of the contribution may be unclear. If they are in charge of teams, for example, they will take certain actions to lead and motivate the team members; the teams will then take actions which will lead towards the desired business results – for example, working to manufacture products, or to sell goods and services. The effects of the managers' actions on the teams, and the teams' actions on business results, may be affected by a variety of other factors – the skills of team members, the activities of the company's competitors, luck, the international exchange rate, and so on. A senior manager who works through other managers will have an even longer causal chain between his or her actions and business results.

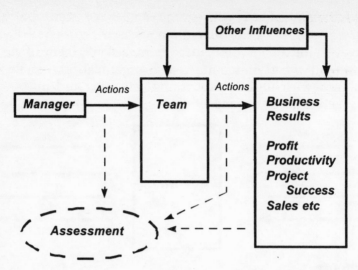

A fair assessment of the ability of an individual manager, therefore, may need to consider outputs of three kinds:

1. the business results achieved by the manager's team;
2. the outputs of the team in attempting to achieve these results;
3. the outputs of the manager in leading team activities.

Ultimately it is the first type of output that is of primary importance to the company, but where the manager's contribution to achieving this output is unclear there is a danger of unfairly rewarding or penalizing individuals by basing all assessment on this measure, without taking into account the other factors which may have influenced the results.

Using the model
Can you identify – for yourself and for the people who work for you – the key outputs that you should achieve? Where it is appropriate, identify the outputs in stages, as in the model, leading ultimately to business results. A new salesperson, for example, might be expected to be able to show established contacts with a target number of prospective purchasers, as an intermediate output leading to the ultimate goal of a certain level of sales.

REFERENCES
For further reading, see Reddin, Bill, *The Output Oriented Manager*, Gower, 1989.

See also model 8.

29. Motivation – the Process

Models of motivation can be divided into process models and content models.

One useful process model is the Porter-Lawler Expectancies model, which sets out the factors that affect performance in the workplace.

Performance is a function of three things: skills, understanding and motivation.

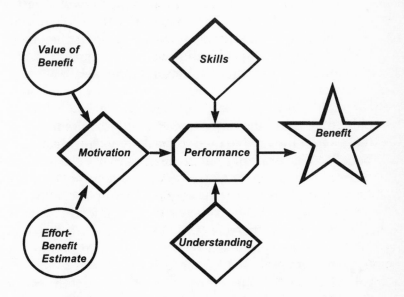

Good performance depends on the person understanding what is required of them, having the skills to achieve what is required, and being motivated to apply the necessary effort.

Poor performance is not necessarily due to a lack of motivation: it might be due to inadequate skills, or an inadequate understanding about what is required.

Motivation to put effort into carrying out a task depends on two major factors:

1. *The expected value of the benefit of carrying out the task.* This benefit could be any kind of return the person may achieve, including monetary gain, personal satisfaction, social status etc. People may also be motivated to avoid disbenefits, or risks and penalties – so on some occasions in the workplace they may put in effort in order to achieve

positive incentives, and in other cases may work hard to avoid negative consequences. (See model 30.)

2. *Whether people think they are likely to be successful in attaining the benefit.* This is based on their estimate of the likelihood of them performing the task successfully, and also whether they think they will receive the benefit if they are successful at the task.

Low motivation may result from people placing a low value on the benefit they expect to get (or are told they will get) from completing the task – relative to the effort that is required. To put it simply, the bonus rate may be too low. Or they may not value the praise and appreciation of their manager, which is likely to follow successful completion of the task.

Low motivation may also result if people think it very unlikely that they will be able to gain the reward – if, for example, they think the task is too difficult for them, or if they feel that even if they completed the task they would not achieve the benefit. For example, in a company which is close to liquidation the workforce may be exhorted to apply more effort, to work harder, in order to keep the company afloat. This attempt to motivate the workers will only be effective with those people who believe there is truly a connection between their hard work and the promised benefit (continued employment). Some people may believe that other factors, outside their control, will have a greater effect on whether or not the company closes (such as decisions made by senior managers and the company's bankers and creditors), and they will not be motivated to work any harder.

Using the model
The model can be used as a simple checklist for managing the performance of the members of your team.

For planning ahead, consider the three factors that affect performance. Do your team members have the necessary skills? Do they understand what is required of them? How are they motivated?

For performance problems, be careful not to assume – without good reason for doing so – that these are the result of poor motivation. Are you sure the person knows what is required? Does he or she have the skills to carry out what is required? There is a significant difference between 'won't do' and 'can't do'.

If it is a motivation problem, this model points to the two main influencing factors. You may be able to increase a person's level of motivation by attention to the value of the benefit, or by reinforcing the belief of the person in their ability to achieve the benefit if they apply effort. Obviously, you are at an advantage if you know what your team members want (i.e. what benefits they value). Reinforcing their belief in their own ability may be a matter of supplying reassurance and boosting their self-confidence. Of course, it is also a matter of setting targets that are in fact within their ability to achieve, and providing enough support and resources for the targets to be reached if the team members play their part.

REFERENCE
Porter, L. W., and Lawler, E. E., *Managerial Attitudes and Performance*, Irwin, 1968.

30. What Motivates People?

In making decisions about how to behave, people are generally motivated by the prospect of achieving some benefit or reward for themselves, and thus satisfying a need. *Benefit* and *reward* are broad ideas which can refer to any kind of satisfying return to the individual, including monetary gain, praise, promotion and social acceptance. People are also motivated to avoid disbenefits – such as discomfort, danger, financial loss, criticism or punishment.

Promising (and providing) benefits and rewards and security from disbenefits is a means of motivation routinely applied in business to employees, customers, suppliers and partners. These promises are perhaps most obvious in the stylized forms of communication adopted in advertising.

Early approaches to motivation in the workplace emphasized the promise of monetary gain (and, to some extent, the threat of punishment) and led to measured work systems and incentive schemes. Later thinking identified a range of possible benefits which individuals may value, including security, praise and appreciation, being accepted in a team, respect, control over their own work, and opportunities to be creative.

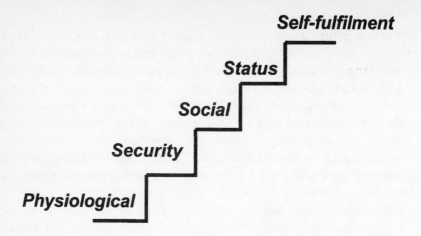

Perhaps the best known model of the diverse benefits that can act to motivate people is Maslow's Hierarchy of Needs. Maslow suggested that people aimed to satisfy needs in a recognized progression, moving from basic needs such as hunger and thirst, up to higher order needs of self-actualization. It is now generally accepted that people do not wait until needs at one level have been satisfied before acting to satisfy needs at a higher level: they may be threatened by insecurity, but still be motivated by social factors, or the desire for autonomy. The framework is a useful reminder, however, of the wide range of benefits that may motivate people.

Another useful and well-known model is Herzberg's Motivation and Hygiene Factors. In a research project, Herzberg identified a range of factors in the workplace that caused dissatisfaction – and therefore lowered motivation – such as low salary, poor job security and bad working conditions. He also identified factors that led to a positive sense of satisfaction – which included a sense of achievement, responsibility and recognition, personal growth and development.

The first group of factors he called the hygiene factors. If these were improved, they no longer caused dissatisfaction, but neither did they cause positive satisfaction. The second group he called the motivation factors. The implications of his model were that managers should consider both types of factors when attempting to motivate staff. Later research has shown, however, that some people appear to work purely in order to make money, and the motivation factors may have little positive effect on them.

Using the models
Both the Maslow and Herzberg models are part of the common parlance of management, and both models should draw our thinking towards considering the range of possible needs that an individual wishes to satisfy in the workplace. It is important, too, to consider this range of needs over different periods of time. Someone may be motivated by the timely word of praise at the conclusion of a job well done; they may also be motivated to work harder and to study by the prospect of acquiring skills and experience that may lead to a better job and more recognition in the future.

As needs exist in different strengths in individuals, you can use the frameworks to categorize the kinds of needs that appear most important to the individual members of your team, and then consider what relevant benefits you can promise and/or provide to satisfy them.

We must take care in attempting to categorize individual needs. The models are intended as aids to understanding what individuals actually want and need – they are not substitutes for this understanding. Our own perceptions of what we need, and what we value, are liable to change over time – and the same is true of most people. Some old needs are satisfied and some new needs arise. What was new, glamorous and attractive last year, and appealed to our need for status (for example, in some jobs the travel and the frequent overnight stays in hotels), can become tedious if there is too much of it. Understanding requires the models to be applied with sensitivity to individual circumstances.

REFERENCE
For summaries of Maslow, Herzberg and other writers on motivation, see Mullins, L., *Management and Organisational Behaviour*, Pitman, 1996 (4th edn), Ch. 14.

31. Theory X and Theory Y

In *The Human Side of Enterprise*, Douglas McGregor compared widely differing sets of assumptions about human nature, and the impact these have on the way we manage others. He suggested that we each may hold one of two contrasting views:

Theory X
People:

Theory Y
people:

- are inherently lazy;
- are self-centred;
- are prepared only to work when this is unavoidable;
- do not want or accept responsibility;
- are resistant to change.

- are naturally inclined to work and enjoy it;
- are self-controlled and internally motivated to work;
- seek rewards in terms of ego satisfaction and self-actualization;
- are willing and able to direct personal effort to a wider good.

Consider how these views get translated into behaviour towards others.

Theory X managers tend to:

- use coercion;
- tightly control their workers through detailed direction and close monitoring;
- see themselves as the boss;
- criticize or offer advice to others.

Theory Y managers tend to:

- promote in others a positive self-motivated willingness to perform;
- stand back and let people get on with the task;
- see themselves as a facilitator or co-ordinator, or as a provider of services and resources to people who work for them;
- empathize with or seek information from others.

McGregor suggested that Theory Y managers get better results, in terms of quality, profit, waste levels, output, labour turnover, problems and innovation, by making use of the unlimited opportunities available at work for personal satisfaction.

Attractive as this sounds, it is clear that there are many managers who we would categorize as Theory X and who are also successful. This may be due to their personal drive and effort, relying less on the results of others. They may also be successful in the short term, moving on before any fundamental and longer-term problems become apparent. Or perhaps their definition of success is narrowly focused.

Using the model
Obviously, Theory X and Theory Y as outlined above are extremes. Most people will fall in between, or show more or less of one or the other according to the circumstances.

It is useful to use the model to reflect on your own practice towards your team: to what extent does your behaviour indicate a Theory X or a Theory Y attitude towards them? Theory X attitudes from managers are likely to promote the kind of behaviour they expect from others: if we treat people as though they are inherently lazy, self-centred and unwilling to accept responsibility, then a certain proportion of them will begin to behave in this way. Similarly, Theory Y attitudes from managers can promote some of their own characteristics in others.

Note that managers with Theory Y attitudes do not present staff with a soft option: on the whole they require more commitment and effort from their staff, but they also provide more of the rewards – not least the satisfaction of achievement, recognition and autonomy. Nor are Theory Y attitudes an unchanging part of a manager's mentality: they are general assumptions about people, which are held to be true until individuals demonstrate otherwise. Some individuals *are* lazy, self-centred and unwilling to accept responsibility: an effective Theory Y manager will not carry them as passengers of the rest of the team.

To explore your values in this area further, you can use a simple self-report questionnaire such as those supplied by Management Learning Resources, which identifies your usual responses to others in key situations. They suggest four categories – critical and advising (Theory X) and empathy and searching (Theory Y). For example:

Identify your most likely response (1–4) to the following statement by someone:

'I work like mad to get rush projects completed! What's my reward for getting them out? Nothing! No thanks, no nothing.

In fact, most of the so-called rush projects sit on people's desks unattended for days.'

You:

1. *'How often does this happen?' (Searching, Theory Y)*
2. *'You ought to tell them that you don't like being treated this way.' (Advising, Theory X)*
3. *'It appears to me you feel like they're taking advantage of you, and that you are being treated unfairly.' (Empathy, Theory Y)*
4. *'You shouldn't get so angry.' (Critical, Theory X)*

There is a clear link here to transactional analysis (see model 4), where critical and advising are Parent behaviours, and empathy and searching are Adult behaviours.

Through analyzing your responses, you can make a conscious choice whether to change your behaviour or not.

REFERENCES
McGregor, Douglas, *The Human Side of Enterprise*, McGraw-Hill, 1960.

Management Learning Resources, PO Box 28, Carmarthen, Dyfed, Wales.

32. *Team Working*

Few of us work alone and few of us can rely solely on our own efforts – most of us work in one or more group settings. Managers in many organizations today express the belief that we should do more than just work in groups – we should work in such a way that the output of a group's collective effort is greater than the sum of its parts. This is real team working.

The benefits of team working are:

- teams are able to tackle bigger jobs than individuals;
- teams generate more ideas and views;
- bringing people together in a team can be a way of addressing common concerns;
- team members provide one another with support and help.

There are a number of models for checking the overall health of a team. We have used a model developed at the Northern Regional Management Centre. Building on the work of Mike Woodcock, it shows effective teams to have these characteristics:

1. Agreed aims and objectives. There is agreement on the overall aims of the team, and individual members are also committed to specific objectives.
2. Review of performance. There is a system for gathering information on how well the team is performing.
3. Agreed roles that complement each other. If everyone plays their part, the team will achieve the desired results.
4. Sound methods for decision-making. There is a good flow of information from the outside world, and there are agreed methods of making decisions within the team.
5. Good communication between team members. Team members are able to talk about problems with one another.
6. Trust and respect. Team members trust and respect one another.
7. Sufficient resources. There are enough resources – including skills – for the tasks in hand.

At the heart of effective team working are clear objectives and agreed common goals. Members depend on each other to achieve the goals to the extent that they openly give each other positive or negative feedback, and also any support and development aid as required to help achieve those goals. Members monitor each other. Performance issues are confronted; conflicts are treated creatively to improve performance. Feedback on team performance – such as measures of team output, and team visibility – are important to the team as a whole, and to its individual members.

Katzenback and Smith identify four levels of team development:

- *pseudo-team* – essentially a team in many ways except that, damagingly, it hasn't yet focused on collective performance (a team without this focus is usually less effective than just a group of individuals);
- *potential team* – a team that has focused on collective performance, but needs sharper team objectives and accountabilities, and better procedures and disciplines;

- *real team* – very similar to our model above;
- *high-performance team* – not only a real team, but one where each member is deeply committed to the personal growth and success of his colleagues

Using the models

You can use the main model to carry out an audit of your team. This can sometimes be a useful collective exercise, creating a questionnaire based on the seven characteristics, and gathering and sharing the opinions of all the team members. From this you may be able to identify the two or three characteristics that are priorities for strengthening.

You may then be able to identify the actions the team might take to improve in the target areas for development, noting the barriers and how you might overcome them.

Be aware that in many managerial and professional situations, team working is not essential – and much is achieved through the application of individual skill and effort. Movement towards greater team working can be treated with distrust by individuals who suspect this will lead to a loss of some of their individual autonomy, and the promotion of greater conformity. In these circumstances, it is vital to achieve the right balance between those areas of the job where individual action is most effective, and those areas where better teamwork is desirable.

REFERENCES

'Building the Team', in *Managing People*, an open learning text published by Newcastle Business School.

Katzenback, J. R. K., and Smith, D. K., *The Wisdom of Teams*, Harvard Business School, 1993.

Woodcock, Mike, *The Team Development Manual*, Gower, 1979.

33. Team Roles

A view of team working made popular by R. Meredith Belbin is that effective teams bring together different contributions from individuals in a productive way. He wrote: 'Teams are a question of balance. What is needed is not well-balanced individuals but individuals who balance well together.' He suggested that while individuals bring different professional abilities to a team, they also may bring different personal skills that can help the team work effectively together, and identified eight team roles that an effective team needs, over and above the functional abilities it requires. These roles enable high-performance team working.

Role	Purpose	Attributes
Shaper	Pushy leader, focus on results	Dynamic, decisive, argumentative, perhaps aggressive and impatient
Co-ordinator	Absorbs alternatives, makes team decisions	Listener, prober, logical, calm, stable, perhaps lacks creativity and can be lazy
Team worker	Promotes harmony, reduces conflict	Sensitive to others, diplomatic, perhaps indecisive
Completer-finisher	Makes the team achieve on time	Professional, conscientious, perhaps too much a perfectionist and worrier
Implementer	Turns team ideas into practice	Organizer, logical, tenacious, perhaps too cautious and resistant to change
Resource investigator	Links to the world outside the team, PR	Communicator, enthusiasm, energy, perhaps poor on evaluation, follow-up and attention to detail
Innovator	Produces creative ideas and proposals	Intelligent, imaginative, unorthodox, perhaps arrogant, vague, isolationist and impractical
Monitor-evaluator	Produces conclusions based on logic and analysis, is practical	Analytical skills, intelligent, anchor, prudent, perhaps a cynic and damper of ideas

A ninth role is that of the specialist – the person who has the specialist knowledge of the area under discussion.

The eight main roles were derived originally from the 16PF test (see model 6). Each role has characteristics which can be seen as strengths and those which can be seen as 'allowable weaknesses'. People have natural preferences for particular roles, and we may each have a profile that indicates a main preference and one or two secondary preferences.

Using the model
Using the 16PF or the simple questionnaire derived by Belbin, identify your preferred roles. As a joint exercise, the Belbin questionnaire can be used to identify the preferred roles of your whole team.

You can then:

- recognize and be sensitive to each other's strengths and weaknesses, and adopt more suitable behaviours to improve relationships within the team;
- identify any gaps in the team as a whole and devise a strategy to fill them, perhaps by co-opting someone else;
- identify team activities where a conscious effort may be needed to see all the roles are carried, perhaps by different people adopting secondary preferences or by introducing systems to regulate team behaviour (e.g. ensuring time-dated action points are placed in the minutes of meetings held by teams with no shapers; ensuring careful checking of results in teams with no completer-finishers);
- bring to the fore the individual(s) whose strengths are needed at any particular stage of a meeting or team task;
- identify your own individual strengths, and build on them, and identify what weaknesses may reasonably be reduced in time.

Belbin suggests that we learn and practise the scripts that are helpful in each role. For example, co-ordinator scripts include:

- *Let's keep the main objective in sight*
- *Has anyone else got anything to add to this?*
- *We like to reach consensus before we move forward, etc.*

Using the Belbin model for team interactions and development can be highly rewarding and make a team significantly more effective. A word of warning, however: because you have a preference for a role it does not mean you have the skills and experience to do it well. A baby has a natural inclination to get up and walk, but there is still a lot of learning to be done. Once you have established your preferences, consider what further skills you might develop.

REFERENCES
Margerison, C. J., and McCann, D., *How to Lead a Winning Team*, MCB University Press, 1984.
Belbin, R., Meredith, *Management Teams: why they succeed or fail*, Butterworth Heinemann, 1981.
Belbin, R., Meredith, *Team roles at work*, Butterworth Heinemann, 1993.

34. Flexible and Self-Managed Teams

Within many organizations in recent years there has been a significant change in the mental models of how people can best work together. The focus has become the team. More responsibility is given to people for how they do their work, and the style of management is directed away from the traditional approach of command and control.

Flexible team working removes the traditional demarcation lines between areas of work. Individuals are trained in more skills, so they are capable of tackling a wider range of tasks, and they are brought together in teams, or 'cells', which contain a wider mixture of abilities than ever before.

The teams take responsibility for producing a product or a service for a customer (internal or external). Typically they become involved in many more stages of the process of production than previously – often including direct contact with external customers.

Companies may take a step beyond flexible team working, and delegate to the teams themselves much more responsibility for making many of the work decisions – creating self-managed teams (SMTs).

SMTs operate with a minimum of direct supervision. For example, given a set of targets, they will usually plan and schedule their own work and make decisions to solve any problems that arise. At the same time the distance between the teams and senior management in the company is often reduced, by reorganizing to remove levels of middle management.

Very good results are claimed for these team-working methods. In terms of productivity, improvements in the order of 25 per cent or more are not unusual.

SMTs have become more common since the mid-1980s. However, a small number of companies have been using SMTs for many years. Procter and Gamble have been using team-working systems since the 1960s: the early results were a saving in manufacturing costs of 30–50 per cent, and at the time the company declared the approach a trade secret, and protected it with the same degree of security as their product design and marketing plans.

There are some simple reasons why the approach should produce improvements in productivity.

1. All the skills are on hand. People are trained to carry out a number of operations to produce a piece of work, so there are fewer delays as components pass from one stage to the next, and fewer communication problems between people working on the same project.
2. With their improved skills, people are better able to identify improvements in how things can be done, and make decisions on how to solve problems. This capability is enhanced where companies take steps to provide teams with sufficient information, and extend the skills training to include business skills and finance skills.
3. As important as the change in ability is the improvement in motivation that comes with greater involvement (see model 31). The work group can also often exert greater influence than a manager over how much effort a person will put into their job.

Flexible team working has sometimes been accompanied by downsizing and de-layering. As people learn more skills, fewer employees may be needed; as they are given more responsibility for managing themselves, the need for managers decreases. This has led to opposition to the introduction of team working, and sometimes a certain amount of cynicism about the more humanitarian messages of empowerment.

Using the model

Introducing SMTs into an organization requires support and understanding at the most senior levels, of course, and a large-scale programme of reshaping working practices, education and training.

Moving to a team-working system is usually more difficult for first line managers than for other people within the organization. They are often very concerned at first about their loss of power and control. They are also faced with two practical challenges: they need to come to a very good understanding of their new role, and they need to learn new skills to perform the new leadership style effectively (see model 26).

Where SMTs have been most effective, companies have set aside time and training resources to help managers to understand their new role and to learn the necessary skills. Where SMTs have been less effective it has sometimes been because managers have not been given this guidance and support in making the transition. They may have been told what *not* to do, but often have not been given the opportunity to learn the new behaviours that will help them to be an effective team leader.

Moving towards a more empowering, facilitative leadership style may be something that you wish to do as an individual manager, regardless of whether this is adopted as a company-wide practice.

Often one of the biggest challenges you will encounter is in making the team face up to difficult decisions. You may need to help the team solve problems, but without directing them to particular answers. Your job can be made much easier if all members of the team have well-developed teamwork skills, particularly in problem analysis, negotiation and communication – and these are areas that may require training and development activities.

REFERENCES

Fisher, Kimball, *Leading Self-Directed Work Teams*, McGraw Hill, 1993.

Manz, Charles C., and Sims, Henry P., *Business Without Bosses*, Wiley, 1993.

Trist, Eric, and Bamforth, K. W., 'Some social and psychological consequences of the longwall method of coal getting', *Human Relations*, 1951, Vol. 4, No. 1.

Wilson, Graham, *Self Managed Team Working*, Pitman, 1995.

See also models 58 and 63.

35. *Team Briefing*

In larger organizations in particular, internal communications are potentially very complex and difficult to manage. Wherever we sit, high or low in the hierarchy, in Function X as opposed to Function Y, we may not always feel we know what is going on. Or if we do, it is through the informal grapevine or our network of contacts, and we hear so many different reports on the same thing it is hard to get an accurate picture.

Team briefing is an attempt to remedy this through a formal system of cascading information down the organization. It works on the assumption that there are discrete groupings or teams at all levels in the organization who can be briefed at the same time in the same way:

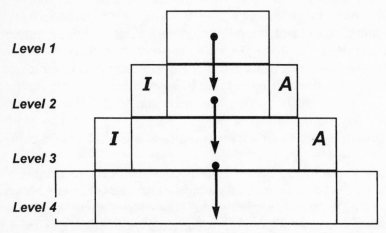

Level 1, for example the production director, formulates the message to be communicated, and passes it directly on to his senior operational managers at Level 2 at one of their regular weekly team briefing meetings. All the Level 2 managers hear the same message at the same time, and can clarify with the Level 1 director and the other Level 2 managers in a group setting what the message means and what the implications might be.

Next, the Level 2 managers need to consider the message and the specific implications for their respective Level 3 unit team leaders. This is a process of interpretation, marked by the 'I' in the model. The Level 2 managers may wish to illustrate the message with relevant examples, or highlight key areas of importance or urgency.

Team briefing schemes usually expect the Level 2 managers to add their own messages, marked by the 'A' in the model, when they pass on the original message. The additions are not so much to do with the original message, but more to do with other messages that originate at their level.

The Level 2 managers next hold a meeting of their Level 3 unit team leaders, and pass on the original message, along with their own messages for onward dissemination. Again, the Level 3 unit team leaders will be able to discuss together with the Level 2 managers the questions and implications.

And so the process downwards continues, with the original message being passed on largely intact, with each layer adding their messages.

This may be what many organizations do naturally, or would like to believe they do. Judging by the regular complaints we hear of poor communication in organizations, such communication may be common sense but it is not common practice. As individuals, we can be forgetful or perhaps incompetent, so a more formal and systematic approach may provide the discipline we need.

Using the model
There are issues to consider in introducing team briefing:

- What training is needed by each layer in the organization? At the very least, presentation skills training may be needed in particular at lower levels of the organization.
- What sort of messages benefit from this structured and potentially time-consuming approach to communication?
- How can we get urgent messages out quickly?
- Are there better ways of communicating organization messages, perhaps using information technology?
- Can the system incorporate an upward stream of information?

If the idea of team briefing appeals to you, it makes sense to estimate whether you have sufficient need for the full formal system, and if so whether the costs of developing it are warranted. How would you measure the benefits of team briefing?

36. Person Specification

Good personnel practice says that we need to define the responsibilities, tasks and performance outputs of a particular job, and
then define the knowledge, skills and competences required to
do it well.

For each task of a particular job, a simple pro-forma might
have the following headings:

Job title:		
Job task:		

Job requirements	Essential	Desirable
Knowledge and skill		
Qualifications		
Personal qualities – aspirations, ambitions, motivation		

If we collate all the specifications together, we will have a
complete and detailed profile of the person needed for the job.

Nowadays, it is not unusual for an organization to draw up
person specifications using a competence model, utilizing either
a standard set of functional performance indicators such as the
Management Standards, or a customized model perhaps
including behavioural characteristics. The value of using such
models is that they can help avoid the vagueness of the terms we
might use, especially when describing personal qualities which
might otherwise be open to a number of interpretations – such
as *initiative*, or *communication skills*.

We need to distinguish with care what is essential and what is
merely desirable – or we may end up with an unrealistic,
idealized specification that no one can meet.

Using the model
The most common use of a person specification is during
recruitment or promotion. Candidates for the job are assessed
against the agreed requirements, and the appointment can be
justified against these agreed criteria.

It may be possible to assess some of the categories in the specification on a simple Yes/No basis (for example, a person will either possess a specified qualification or not). In many cases, however, the characteristics in the specification may be demonstrated to a greater or lesser degree, and it is best to use a simple scale to express the differences between candidates.

For example:

3 – exceeds what is required
2 – meets what is required and is better than average
1 – meets what is required but seems below average
0 – does not meet what is required

Some characteristics may be more important for the job than others, and this can be represented by giving different weightings to the requirements laid out in the specification. In this simple example, Jim and Jane are candidates for the same job. For purposes of illustration, we focus on only three requirements, each of which has been weighted to reflect its relative importance to the job.

Requirements	Weight (10)	Rating (10) Jim	Rating (10) Jane	Score Jim (W×R)	Score Jane (W×R)
Knowledge of market	6	5	8	30	48
Product knowledge	3	2	5	6	15
Ability to sell products	9	9	3	81	27
TOTAL				117	90

In this example, Jane knows more about the market and has better knowledge of the product, but Jim is much better at selling. Since selling ability is far more important in this job, then Jim should get it. Of course, Jane might be able to learn to sell, just as Jim will certainly be expected to learn more about the market and products. In any decisions about recruitment or promotion, you have to make judgements about the ability of candidates to learn the required skills.

By specifying a range of characteristics needed in order to perform a job, and assessing each candidate against each characteristic in a systematic way, person specifications can be a powerful shield against halo or horns effects – the way in which our perception of a person can be coloured by a strong positive attribute (the halo effect) or a strong negative one (the horn effect). The same principles are applied in systematic approaches to identifying development needs (see model 15).

Using weighted scoring scales is a useful way of comparing the assessments of the different members of a panel of interviewers – although it is usual for the final figures to inform the decision, rather than to dictate it.

37. Skills Grids

The skills grid is a simple and effective method for a manager to summarize the skills needed and the skills possessed by their team.

The first stage is to identify the skills needed by your team. The backbone of the list may be obvious technical skills; there may also be skills and competences set out by the company appraisal system. Other skills might be interpersonal – such as those related to customer care, or to the ability to work co-operatively and supportively with other team members, or aspects of supervisory skills. Other skills may concern aspects of individual effectiveness – such as time management, pro-activity, good judgement.

The next stage is to assess the extent to which your team members possess each skill. For this some form of rating system is required: a scale of 1–5 is often sufficient, or simply a three-level scale of high, medium and low. It is also useful to estimate the extent to which each of your team members needs to possess the skill. These needs may be indicated by the individual's position and responsibilities – the more senior members of the team may need more supervisory skills, for example, and be expected to show more initiative.

The grid can provide an overview of the collective strengths and development needs of the team – and the same for each individual member. It may show up individual priorities for development, and also highlight areas where the team as a whole is currently weak.

As an example, this extract from a grid shows two members of a team of trainers, and the skills they possess and need.

	Ann	Bill	
Research	H / H	M / L	
Consulting	H / H	M / L	
Lectures	M / L	M / H	
Workshops	M / M	M / H	
Tutorials	M / M	M / M	
Leadership	H / M	L / L	
Marketing	H / H	M / L	
			Have / Need

Using the model

There are a number of choices to be made if you decide to use the skills grid. Should it be openly available to your whole team? Or should it be a planning tool for your own reference? Should it contain all the key skills needed by the team, or only a selection of them?

Where the grid is open to view by the whole team, issues of mutual disclosure, assessment and motivation are likely to arise. If, for example, you rate a senior member of the team as low in supervisory skills, it may not help either the individual or the team to have this displayed for all to see. In most cases we have seen where a skills grid is on public display, it has been restricted to technical skills, and most often in fact to inputs – with the titles of training courses in place of descriptions of the skills. These grids are uncontroversial: there is no need for a high, medium or low grade – either the person has attended the course or they have not. These records of training can be interesting, and there may be a good case for using them as public documents within the team to focus attention on a new area for training – such as being able to use new IT systems, or having been trained in new procedures – but they are not so revealing as an overall assessment of abilities.

There are therefore advantages in keeping the skills grid as a confidential document, a private overview or shorthand of the abilities of your whole team, while directing your efforts towards the priority areas that it indicates. There is no reason why your assessment of each person's strengths and development needs should not be shared with that individual, but sharing each person's profile with the whole team can often create problems.

As an overview document, it is usually helpful to limit the length of the list of skills. The value of the grid in providing a summary of strengths and needs can be negated by too much detail – and creating a very detailed – and accurate – grid will also often be very time-consuming. However, creating an accurate and useful grid is not a quick job. If you want the grid to be helpful in assessing all key strengths and development needs, be sure to reflect on exactly what knowledge and skills are really required to produce good results. This inevitably means doing more than noting the easily identifiable technical skills – you must also try to define the interpersonal skills and the personal effectiveness elements, too. Building up your list over several days, reflecting on the skills and abilities of the best members of your team in each task area, is often the most effective way to produce a worthwhile grid.

Finally, follow up your assessment with an action plan. There may be some needs affecting the whole team, some affecting only one or two members, and some which are unique to particular individuals. You are unlikely to be able to address every need within a twelve-month period – unless your team is very small and/or very experienced and skilful – so you will need to prioritize. Update your assessments periodically – because needs change and people develop.

References
See also models 7, 15, 19 and 36.

38. The Training Triangle

The three partners in the triangle of work-related learning and training are the learner, the trainer and the learner's line manager. Rationally, these partners should work together to help the individual develop the skills and knowledge the organization needs. However, this is often a relationship characterized by conflict and lack of communication.

The major breakdown in communication tends to be between

the trainer and the line manager: problems can arise here through conflicts of interest and lack of understanding.

Line managers may complain about the lack of relevance of the training and the insularity of the trainers. For their part, trainers may grumble about the negative attitudes and the lack of support and participation of the line managers.

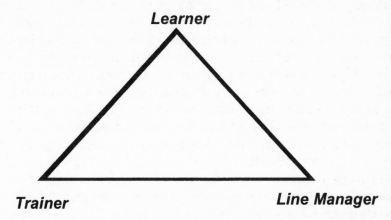

Both are in some respects competing for a precious resource – the learner's time. Both may have different ideas about where the learner should direct their time and effort. The line manager may acknowledge their responsibility for helping the learner to develop the skills he/she will need tomorrow, but they are also very often under pressure to produce results today – a pressure which they partly pass on to learners in terms of workload and deadlines.

Where they are committed to training and development, line managers may hold firm views about the development needs of their staff. Trainers, lacking the experience of working with the individual learner, and perhaps limited by the resources at their disposal to develop personalized training programmes, may pursue a set of more general learning objectives.

Learners arrive on training and development programmes for a variety of reasons – from the person who wants to acquire knowledge and skills so that she can move to another job (perhaps even to another company), to the person who has been sent on the course by his line manager (perhaps more in hope than expectation that the training course will solve a performance problem). They can suffer if the trainers are out of touch and the training is irrelevant, and they can also suffer if their line manager is unsupportive.

Using the model

The model describes the framework of a set of relationships which have the potential for conflict. Better communication will not necessarily resolve all of the underlying tensions between the potentially different aims and interests of the three parties, but an open discussion of priorities for learning and development is often helpful.

The training departments in many organizations take steps towards this by requiring comments from line managers, both before and after the learner attends a training course, on the benefit they expect the learner to derive from the training, and the results that have in fact been achieved. More comments from learners are also often sought.

Negotiated learning contracts, agreed between the three parties, are frequently used in work-based training programmes, providing a structure for the discussion of priorities, objectives and action plans.

The underlying tension will persist, however, if the three parties have difficulty reaching agreement on what the learner should be learning. Resolving the tension will depend in part on the context in which the training programme is provided. Is it intended to address current (or at least short-term) training needs? Or is it part of a longer-term programme of development? In these circumstances, whatever your position in the training triangle, your skills of persuasiveness will have at least a little influence on how far you are able to achieve your aims.

REFERENCES

Boak, George, *A Complete Guide to Learning Contracts*, Gower, 1998.

See also models 19, 41, 42 and 44.

39. Coaching

There is a growing view that managers and leaders must behave as coaches to their staff. Coaching is a complex process, with different forms and purposes.

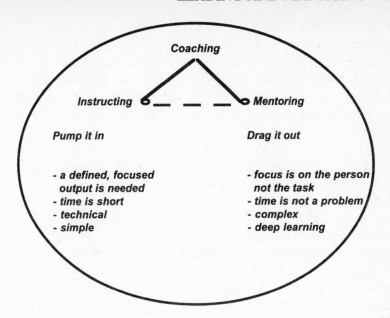

This model shows coaching as having two legs, instructing and mentoring.

Instructing is suitable when time is short and a defined standard has to be reached for the task at hand. It is often used for simpler technical tasks that can be repeated in the same way by different people. More complex tasks can usually be broken down into simple ones, and the instructor focuses on one at a time. The instructor-coach can 'pump in' knowledge and skills.

Mentoring usually focuses on the person rather than the task. It often requires time since the approach is more reflective and individualized. The mentor-coach uses questions to 'drag out' what the individual is thinking and to encourage alternative ways of seeing things. A mentor is perhaps best seen as a facilitator of a person's development, but not responsible for it. Learning is usually much deeper, helping to shape values and beliefs.

Coaches may use both pumping in and dragging out on occasions. These activities may be mixed in one session, with the coach stepping from one mode to the other.

Good coaches consider three things: the inputs, the outputs and the process.

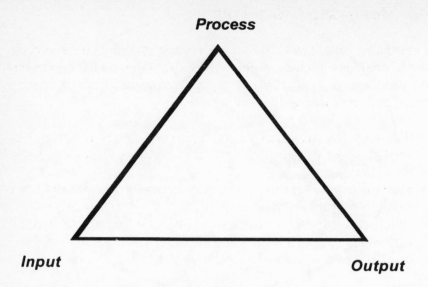

- *Inputs:* the knowledge and skills to be presented to the learner
- *Outputs:* the level of performance to be attained
- *Process:* the delivery processes – which may be one-to-one discussions, lectures, practical exercises, groupwork, etc.

Using the models
When acting as a coach, consider the dimensions of mentoring/ instructing, and assess the balance that is required in your situation. You may find yourself disposed to one style of coaching rather than the other, and it helps to check whether your natural inclination is what is required in the circumstances. Instructing often feels easier for first-time coaches, because it is less interactive and the coach feels more in control – but some of the mentoring approach may be more effective. And most coach-mentors will at times see the benefit in providing some input of facts, frameworks or ideas.

It is helpful to have in mind the inputs, outputs and processes in a coaching situation. In some circumstances, the outputs and/or inputs may be clearly defined – there may be performance standards the person must reach, there may be a prescribed syllabus. From these starting points the most effective process can be derived. Sometimes, however, the process is the starting point: in experiential learning, the aim is to generate opportunities to have new experiences, and to learn from them, without there necessarily being a clear idea of outputs or inputs.

40. Modifying Behaviour

Peter Honey has produced an interesting model of how we can try to change someone else's behaviour. When someone causes us problems at work, Honey argues we usually adopt one or more of the following lines of action:

- discount the problem – by trying to make it seem un-important, or adopting the position that everything has been done to no avail;
- give a pep talk – if the person is working for us, we might tell them to pull their socks up;
- coach or appraise – develop or train the person to behave differently, or even send them away for training;
- punish – in a variety of ways.

Honey argues that these approaches may have varying degrees of success in the short term, but are often ineffective in the longer term.

One might say that in order to change a person's behaviour, we need to identify the causes, usually internal ones – their feelings, values and motives. The behaviour is just a symptom of an underlying cause. However, trying to tackle deep-rooted feelings, values and motives can be risky, and may best be left to skilled counsellors and psychiatrists.

Honey suggests we should focus on the behaviour as the problem rather than just a symptom, and identify the external influences that trigger the behaviour. He uses this model for behaviour modification (BMod):

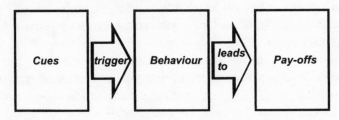

Adapted from Peter Honey, 1980

In this model, the cue is the trigger. It could be a word, or an action, something that sets off the behaviour. The pay-off is the climax or reward that follows the behaviour.

Honey says we need to tackle both the cues of the undesired

behaviour and the pay-offs. Change the cue and we change the behaviour. Changing the pay-offs can be even more powerful.

Cues are only part of the reason why we do something. Through experience, we also learn what the consequences of our behaviour are, and we are able then to anticipate the probable pay-off next time the behaviour is about to be demonstrated. An example: if a worker doesn't do a particular task well, the boss might not give the task to him/her again. The pay-off is the 'reward' of avoiding doing the task. If the task was an unpleasant one in the first place, then avoiding the task in the future really is a reward.

How often do we reward the bad worker by not giving him work, and punish the good worker by giving him extra?

Using the model
BMod may appear rather mechanical, but it does provide a structured way of trying to change someone's behaviour for the better. It is a realistic approach; it is not overly ambitious in attempting to tackle deep-seated values or beliefs, or a lifetime's baggage.

To use the model:

1. When you identify some undesired behaviour, identify the cues – not the 'causes', but the cues external to the person – that trigger the behaviour. Behaviour is no accident; there is always a cue.
2. Identify the pay-offs for the undesired behaviour, especially those that are likely to encourage the behaviour to be continued with similar cues.
3. Identify what behaviour you actually want the person to demonstrate in the circumstances.
4. Identify what cues and pay-offs you can change and decide upon a strategy.
5. The next time a situation that normally triggers the behaviour is likely to arise, make some changes to the cues and/or the pay-offs.

Very often this may mean making small changes to your own behaviour to avoid triggering or rewarding the behaviour of the other person which you want to change.

REFERENCE
Honey, Peter, *Solving People Problems*, McGraw-Hill, 1980.

Change

The pace of change within organizations over the past ten years has been unrelenting. Economic and technological factors have combined to bring dramatic pressure to bear on products, services and working methods. Peter Vaill has coined the analogy of *continuous white water* as an image of today's managerial task. If the old model of change viewed white water as the occasional rapids which interrupt the normally smooth, stable flow of a river, Vaill has pictured the managerial task as the continuous negotiation of rapids. The old model of change – featuring a period of flux and confusion as an interlude between two states of stability – is no longer deemed appropriate.

In reality, there is almost always resistance to pressures to change. There are those who, for various reasons, want to maintain the current state of affairs – and those who favour change, but not in the direction that is proposed. In the late 1970s, Donald Schon described the patterns of *dynamic conservatism* – the ways in which people within organizations attempt to minimize, divert and neutralize pressures to change. However, some of the radical changes in organizations in the decades that have followed – particularly downsizing, right-sizing, de-layering, restructuring, re-engineering – have been sufficiently forceful to overcome many of the defences of dynamic conservatism.

The comprehensive change initiatives common within larger corporations – in areas such as quality improvement, empowerment, team working, performance improvement and other measures intended to change the corporate culture – are understandable attempts by senior managers to influence large numbers of employees. Where one initiative is rapidly succeeded by another, however, and where the gaps between the espoused theory of the initiative and the actual behaviour of its promoters are wide and frequent, the dominant simple model becomes one of a *bandwagon, latest management fad* or, colloquially, the *flavour of the month*. In some organizations, people are now resistant to change through *change fatigue*, rather than through preference for a stable way of life that is threatened by disruption.

From a more detached perspective, the shape of change

through some of these initiatives resembles the swing of a pendulum: the image is of a gathering momentum in one direction, moving further towards an extreme, before slowing down, stalling and reversing to the opposite extreme. When the pendulum within a company swings towards greater decentralization, for example, it is tempting to predict that within a few years it will swing back towards greater central-ization, or when the swing is towards establishing systems and procedures to bet that within a few years the movement will be back towards developing and empowering people.

There are a number of other simple images in common use to describe the nature and the pace of change. We speak of *revolutionary* and *evolutionary* changes, usually when we are advocating the latter over the former, and representing evolution as a gradual, incremental development which is in harmony with what has gone before. Yet many of our images of change concern a sharp shift in the state of affairs, rather than a gentle progression.

A *step change* represents a point where a situation suddenly alters. It may be in a profile of costs, in the improvement of a skill, or in output.

A step change in performance may be achieved when a *critical mass* is reached – a certain volume of customers or clients who support the company, or a certain number of shareholders who oppose the board, or a certain number of employees who will support the change programme.

Situations may remain more or less unchanged until they pass a *trigger point* – a majority on this committee or that board, the support of this or that key individual, or the final straw that in the fable was enough to break the camel's back.

The pace of change may move in other ways – fears have been expressed since the 1960s about *exponential changes* in the deterioration of the environment, multiplier effects produce exponential change in the performance of economies, and market growth can follow an exponential curve.

Change and reform can be reactions to problems in the current state of affairs, and desires are often expressed for a complete and ideal solution to the problem – the images of the *magic rabbit* or the *magic bullet* express the lack of realism of such desires. Often political pressures for change preclude the thorough analysis and comprehensive consultation that problems deserve – and powerful stakeholders push for a *quick fix*.

Many of the individuals with whom we have worked have been engaged in trying to change their organizations. Some of these changes have been large-scale company-wide realignments, others have been more modest attempts to alter and improve – often made more difficult by entrenched attitudes and influential opposition.

Useful simple models are those which contrast the perspectives the protagonists take: to the change agent, a set of facts may represent a *problem* – an unsatisfactory state of affairs, with negative consequences, about which something can and should be done. Others may view the same set of facts as simply a *situation* – perhaps an unsatisfactory state of affairs, but one which must be accepted and endured. The contrast between problem and *opportunity* – and the ability to see opportunities in problems – is probably more often talked about than actually evidenced, but where it can be put into practice it is nonetheless a powerful reversal of a dominant perception.

Continuous improvement is a model of a state of mind that is in some organizations more espoused than actual. Its opposite is, in the vernacular, the guideline: *If it ain't broke, don't fix it.*

In the conflicts between change agents and those who would maintain stability, and between agents of different changes, in the discussions, compromises and collaborations which ensue, the simple model of attempting to achieve *win-win* outcomes (as opposed to the zero-sum model of win-lose) has a certain attractive currency.

Most of the models on the following pages concern key aspects of how to bring about change – a process which involves persuasion, inspiration, the winning of commitment, and success in organizational politics, as people step beyond the boundaries of their current role and attempt to act as leaders rather than as managers.

Some of the models in other sections of this book are also very relevant to managing change. Transformational leadership (see model 24) is founded on the notion of a leader as a change-maker. This type of leadership depends on creativity (see model 13) and assertiveness (see models 1 and 2). To inspire others we need to understand what motivates them as individuals (see models 29, 30 and 31) as well as how they act collectively (see model 52) and how they may respond to strategic change (see model 49). As we work through the surprises that change often has in store, we also need analytical skills (see models 67,

68 and 69), as well as an understanding of how to learn in new situations (see models 15–23).

In recent years there have been many changes towards directions represented by other models in this book – for example, greater empowerment (model 34), the customer concept (model 63) and the learning organization (model 58).

Bringing about change in organizations is rarely a simple matter. The change agents with whom we have worked have often acted to champion changes that have represented steps into the unknown. As Rosabeth Moss Kanter has written: 'Everything looks like a failure in the middle. In nearly every change project doubt is cast on the original vision because problems are mounting and the end is nowhere in sight.' We have found the models that follow to be helpful in managing these situations.

41. Force Field Analysis
42. Process Model of Persuasion
43. Sliding Scale of Objectives
44. Common Ground
45. Eight Steps to Organizational Change
46. Networks, Coalitions and Change
47. Political Skills for Managers
48. Stakeholder Analysis

REFERENCES
Kanter, Rosabeth Moss, 'Improving the acceptance and use of new technology: organizational and inter-organizational challenges', in *People and Technology in the Workplace*, ed. Kanter, National Academy of Engineering, Washington DC, 1991.
Schon, Donald, *Beyond the Stable State*, Jossey-Bass, 1979.
Vaill, Peter, *Managing as a Performing Art*, Jossey-Bass, 1990.

41. Force Field Analysis

Force field analysis (FFA) is a simple but effective model for analysing the factors for and against a proposed change. It can be used on a micro scale, to quickly identify the different arguments that are put forward in a discussion, or on a macro scale to assess the whole range of factors that an individual or group should take into account when deciding whether or not to change their position.

Driving Forces   **_Restraining Forces_**

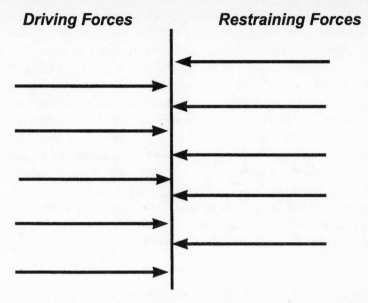

The separate factors are identified as driving forces or restraining forces, and their relative strength is estimated. The model can then be used to weigh up a decision, or to develop a strategy for persuading other parties.

If you favour change in a particular situation, for example, you would identify the driving and the restraining forces, and then:

* plan how to strengthen existing driving forces, or to add new driving forces;
* plan how to weaken or remove restraining forces.

In using the model to persuade other people, it can also be helpful to identify open and hidden forces.

Open forces are those factors that can (and probably will) be discussed and debated. In any proposal for change, for example, the costs of the change and any financial benefits (increased revenue or decreased costs over time) are typical topics for discussion. The costs may be seen as excessive (in which case they are a strong restraining force), or as reasonable and justifiable (in which case they are only a weak restraining force). The expected financial benefits are a driving force. Costs, even reasonable ones, are almost always a restraining force – the only exception being those times when a budget must be spent urgently before the end of the financial year.

Hidden forces are those factors that may influence the

outcome, but will generally not be discussed. For example, suppose that you are making a proposal for change to your boss and suppose your boss is someone who doesn't like change – whose unspoken motto is 'Let sleeping dogs lie', or, 'If it ain't broke, don't fix it'. This is a restraining force on your proposal that you should take into account. In the case of the financial open forces, above, it is important to be prepared with information about costs and benefits. In the case of these hidden forces, it is helpful to have a strategy to combat them: either a very powerful driving force ('There is no alternative but to make some change here' or 'The managing director has said we have to do this now') or a weakening of the restraining force ('This doesn't involve much change' and 'This is really just continuing what we have already been doing').

Using the model

FFA is one of the most effective tools for influencing change. It can help you to set out the factors that are likely to be important, and to prepare your strategies for persuasion. It is also sufficiently simple for you to use it in the middle of meetings, to capture and summarize arguments as they are made.

FFA provides a warning not to concentrate too much on your own viewpoints and arguments, but also to consider the contradictory standpoint.

More experienced and effective persuaders spend time identifying the forces that oppose them, and assessing how to weaken, neutralize or accommodate them.

Although FFA encourages you to identify a range of forces that will support your position, in practice it is usually not advisable to stress them all in your argument. 'There are six good reasons why we should adopt this scheme' may sound convincing at first – but if you are facing opposition to your proposal you are inviting an attack on the weakest of your 'good reasons'. It may, therefore, be wiser to lead with the strongest one, two or three reasons, where you are truly confident, and press with them at every opportunity.

REFERENCE
Lewin, Kurt, *Field Theory in Social Science*, Harper, 1951.

42. Process Model of Persuasion

The process of persuading other people to accept and support change can be broken into stages. A number of models have attempted to identify these stages.

One of the simplest and most effective is the three-part un-freezing-shaping-refreezing model of Kurt Lewin, which particularly addresses the way people's attitudes may change towards an issue.

Lewin's three stages can be summarized as:

Unfreezing
At the outset a person's attitude towards a particular issue may be fairly fixed and 'frozen'. Before they will change their mind, these attitudes must first be unfrozen. For example, suppose they are happy and contented with the way a system currently operates, whereas you wish to bring about a change. Unless you do some work to 'unfreeze' this attitude, they will be resistant to any of your proposals.

Shaping
In this stage a number of different strategies may be followed as the person seeks a new perspective on the situation. There are opportunities to promote your proposal.

Refreezing
It is important to win some gesture of commitment to your proposal as a movement towards fixing, or refreezing the person's attitude. This is necessary if you are going to be able to proceed with their support.

Most other process models are more complex than this, yet we have found this three-part structure to be a valuable source of insight into bringing about change.

Using the model
The model can be used at micro and at macro levels of changing attitudes – in other words, from using the framework for briefly discussing a proposal with an individual, to using it to shape a company-wide change process.

Typically, to unfreeze a person's attitude to the present state of affairs, you first point out problems and difficulties. These may be apparent now, or they may be expected to have an impact in the future.

The person you are trying to persuade may:

- be unaware of the problems and difficulties, or unaware of the extent of them, or their consequences;
- be unaware that the situation could be improved;
- see improving this system as a lower priority than making other changes.

The reverse approach is to point out opportunities that may exist, and benefits that may result, from making a change: sometimes people are more moved by the idea of solving problems, and sometimes they are more moved by the idea of seizing opportunities.

The extent of the necessary unfreezing will vary. The person may be very willing to consider possible changes – or may be very committed to the current position. Generally, there is little point in continuing to the shaping stage of the process unless you have been successful in unfreezing the current position.

Shaping may mean simply putting forward your proposal in a persuasive way, setting out the advantages and showing how they outweigh the expected costs or risks. It may, however, also entail inviting participation and contributions from the other party, and building these into the proposal. At the macro level, in company-wide change processes, it may involve considerable investment in time and effort in helping people to become familiar with the proposals, allowing discussion and debate on them, and perhaps amending the detail of them as a result of consultation.

Freezing means winning commitment to or approval of your proposal. Clear signs of commitment can include:

- a signature on a cheque, or on a budgetary authorization;
- a public statement of support for your proposal (the more public the better).

If it is not possible to achieve these, you may have to settle for:

- a statement that your proposal will be supported if certain conditions are met (e.g. if proposed costs are reduced, or if results elsewhere are above a certain level of return);

- a statement agreeing that the current situation is undesirable, and that something should be done – and your proposal will be considered along with a number of other options.

In these last two examples, refreezing is occurring, but not in the ideal shape to support your proposal. You need to judge whether if the situation can be kept in a fluid state it will be to your advantage in the longer run, or whether the shape of this commitment is the best you might expect.

Applying the model means having a strategy for each of the phases, and having an awareness of when one phase is moving (or should be nudged along) into another.

REFERENCES

Lewin, Kurt, *Field Theory in Social Science*, Harper, 1951.

For a good example of the use of Lewin's model at a macro level see Johnson, Gerry, and Scholes, Kevan, *Exploring Corporate Strategy*, Prentice Hall, 1997 (4th edn), Ch. 11.

43. Sliding Scale of Objectives

In putting forward proposals for change, it is sometimes easy to take too simple a view.

We make a request, or a proposition, and hope it will be accepted along the lines we have suggested. We may be prepared for: (a) acceptance; or (b) rejection. Our proposition might be represented as a simple, narrow target:

Our target ------------------ ☐

However, the response may be not so simple. The other person would like to help us, would love to co-operate, but is unable to provide what we want in quite the shade of blue we have requested, or at the exact time we need it, or at the cost we want to pay. It might be possible to provide something in red, a little smaller, at the time we want. Or a yellow one, cheaper, a day later.

As we listen to this response we realize that a more effective view of our target would have been as a range of possibilities, from the minimum acceptable, to the ideal, with what we realistically expect to achieve somewhere in the middle:

Minimum   Target   Ideal

Based on Kennedy et al., 1984.

This idea of a range of objectives is obvious in formal negotiating situations, such as industrial relations bargaining, or sales contracts. In these circumstances, one party's ideal position may be close to another party's minimum acceptable point – and many of the key terms are quantifiable, because they involve money.

In most proposals for change, there are quantifiable elements: money (how much financial support/investment will you give this proposal?) and time (when will it start, how long will it go on?). There may also be other resource elements which can be quantified – (how many people/computers/regions will you give me for the project?), as well as quantifiable targets – (what rate of return must the project achieve?).

The diagram is still too simple as it stands for all but the most basic of negotiations, because in most situations there will be a number of issues, each with a notional ideal, target and minimum point, but which may be traded off against one another.

We have already indicated some of the likely issues, above: how much investment; when can we begin, how long can we take, what other resources will be available; what rate of return is required.

Other issues might include the level of management support: ideal might be clear public support from very senior management, requiring everyone to co-operate with us; minimum might be a private statement of support – and we have to go ahead and persuade others to co-operate with us.

The degree of acceptance is likely to be an issue: an ideal position may be for our proposal to be adopted permanently, throughout the company, right away. We may have to settle for a trial period, in one department, in the first instance.

The degree of control or discretion might be another issue: we want to have sole charge of the project, reporting on progress to the deputy managing director. We might have to settle for reporting to the operations manager, who will have nominal control on a day-to-day basis.

Using the model
The model can be particularly useful in three respects:

- encouraging thoughts about the variety of issues that may be present in any proposal, rather than viewing a proposal as a seamless package;
- encouraging thoughts about the range of possible outcomes for each issue;
- encouraging thoughts about trade-offs between issues, and the relative attraction of different packages.

For example, would you prefer to have sole control over a three-month pilot programme in one department, or report to the operations manager as part of a company-wide scheme? The model does not provide an answer to this question – because the answer will depend on your own priorities – but it might help you to identify this package and allow you time to weigh your priorities.

In advance of presenting a proposal – or while you are preparing a case for one – note the characteristics of what you want (these will be the issues) and for each characteristic consider a range of possibilities – these may be a sliding scale, if they can be counted, such as money or time, or possibilities that are different in kind (e.g. the project will be located in the operations department, the finance department, the marketing department or the chief executive's office).

Use the best information available to you to check out the likelihood of each of these possibilities: the model is not a substitute for good intelligence. Think about your preferences, and sound out the chances of success of a proposal that is somewhere between what you expect and the ideal, to allow room for manoeuvre and still produce something that is acceptable.

REFERENCE
Kennedy, Gavin, Benson, John, and McMillan, John, *Managing Negotiations*, Hutchinson Business Books, 1984 (2nd edn).

For a range of good ideas on negotiation see Fisher, R., and Ury, W., *Getting to Yes*, Arrow, Random House, 1997.

44. Common Ground

The idea of common ground, or mutual interest, is a helpful one in a wide range of situations. In contemplating a change to the current situation, for example, it is useful to consider areas where we may be in agreement with others whose support might be of value. In face-to-face negotiations with others there is likely to be some common ground, and it is worth spending time identifying it – although there may be a strong temptation to focus on those issues where we are trying to bring about some movement in their position. Those issues need attention and assessment, of course, but common ground will form the basis of any agreements that we build with others, and we should spend time mapping it out and discussing it with them.

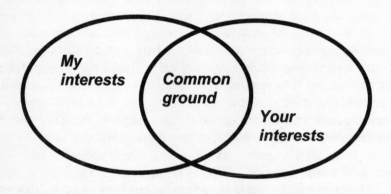

This model is not only of use for the negotiations that may arise when we are trying to implement changes; it can also be of help in identifying proposals for new projects, and developing networks of relationships. In relation to customers, we can consider what changes we might make to the way we provide them with services. What can we do that will benefit them? What can we do that will benefit us? What can we do that is in our mutual interest?

Based on Stumpf and Mullen, 1992.

A development of this model is to add a third consideration, of our capabilities or resources: what can we do? This brings an element of relative practicality into the equation. There are many things that we *might* do, in the mutual interest of ourselves, our customers and our colleagues – but what can we offer that we can provide out of our own resources?

Using the model
A simple use of this mental model is to check on whether you tend to focus on the differences or the similarities between your views and the views of others, between your interests and the interests of other people with whom you work. Identifying and understanding differences and similarities is a sign of an active intelligence – but people can show a predilection towards one type of understanding to the detriment of the other, and it is worth reflecting on your own thinking and identifying any such tendency.

Too great a focus on differences and you are unable to identify common ground; too great a focus on similarities and you are inclined to see common ground where it does not exist.

As well as in negotiations about changes, the model can be used proactively to develop your networks. You may consider:

• how others can help you achieve what you want;

- what information, support, resources you can provide in a helpful way to other people;
- what mutual projects you might tackle together.

REFERENCE
Stumpf, S. A., and Mullen, T. P., *Taking Charge*, Prentice Hall, 1992.

45. Eight Steps to Organizational Change

John Kotter has identified an eight-step model for leading effective organizational change. The model is addressed at large-scale organizational transformation, but it contains lessons for changes of a more modest nature, too.

1. *Establish a sense of urgency.* Examine the company's situation. Identify and discuss major threats or opportunities. Communicate this information in ways that will have impact on others within the company, getting their attention and paving the way for winning co-operation.
2. *Form a powerful guiding coalition.* Build a group with enough power to lead the change and help the group to work together as a team. A group of no more than five people may be effective in steering a moderate change exercise, but Kotter notes that for major change in a large organization a group of 20–50 people will be needed to ensure effective implementation.
3. *Create a vision.* A picture of the future that can be communicated relatively easily to stakeholders will help direct the change exercise. Kotter notes: 'In failed transformations, you often find plenty of plans and directives and programs, but no vision.'
4. *Communicate the vision.* Use every means possible to communicate the new vision and strategies for change, and to capture the hearts and minds of the people within the organization who must be convinced of the value of change. Communication includes acting as a role model and teaching new behaviours by example.
5. *Empower others to act on the vision.* This step may include helping others to understand how they can take action to achieve the change, and encouraging them to move forward.

It can also include amending systems or structures that provide serious obstacles to change.

6. *Create short-term wins.* Plan and achieve visible improvements in performance and reward people who achieve the improvements. Without these short-term wins, people will become disheartened and dismotivated.

7. *Consolidate and build.* Use the credibility created by the short-term gains to make further changes to systems, structures and policies that are creating obstacles. Don't celebrate victory too soon – this will reduce motivation too quickly and the change effort may fizzle out. Find new specific projects and new targets to add novelty and energy to the process.

8. *Institutionalize the new approaches.* Build the new approaches into the basic systems, structures and culture of the organization.

Using the model
Kotter developed this model out of his experiences of the mistakes he had observed in managers attempting to bring about major changes in their organizations. We have seen managers use this model successfully to structure their attempts to change aspects of the way their company operates.

Kotter is insistent on the need to respect each step and phase of the model: 'Skipping steps creates only the illusion of speed and never produces a satisfying result . . . critical mistakes in any of the phases can have a devastating impact, slowing momentum and negating hard-won gains.'

You might use the model to support ideas you have for changing your organization. How would you go about the first four steps of the model? What does your vision look like? How can you communicate it in a way that will have maximum impact? Who can you work with, as allies in a coalition?

REFERENCES
Kotter, John, 'Leading Change: Why Transformation Efforts Fail', *Harvard Business Review*, March-April 1995.

See also model 24.

46. Networks, Coalitions and Change

A number of writers and researchers have focused on the role of networks and coalitions in bringing about change. For example, Rosabeth Moss Kanter believes that networking is an important activity for achieving change. According to Kanter, in order to achieve change managers need three 'power tools':

- information;
- support;
- resources.

In most cases, managers do not have enough of these at their command to achieve significant changes, and therefore they must seek them through the networks they create. She found many examples of successful 'intrapreneurs' operating in this way in middle management positions within large corporations.

In an invaluable study of the use of networks, which includes original research and also extensive summaries of work carried out by other writers, Kaplan and Mazique found that effective managers are likely to network with people at all levels, as a means of trading information and support. The managers who were most successful in doing this were flexible and adaptable, able to understand the interests and values of a wide range of people, and able to mix with others in a spirit of give and take.

John Kotter, whose work is quoted extensively in Kaplan and Mazique (1983), is another writer who has studied the importance of networks and coalitions (see model 45).

Kanter's intrapreneurs spent a great deal of time exploring and discussing the area where they were considering change, and in the process lining up supporters for the project, drawn mainly from peers, managers of related functions, stakeholders in the matter, potential collaborators – usually through informal, one-to-one meetings – before a formal proposal was developed and put forward to senior management for approval.

Using the models
Many of the most effective managers with whom we have worked have displayed an instinctive understanding of the importance of networks and coalitions in the change process, and demonstrated skill and consideration in relating to the people with a stake in the change – including members of their

own team, more senior managers, colleagues, customers and suppliers.

Many of the less experienced managers with whom we have worked, however, have a more wary, less positive view of networks. They half expect decisions on change to be made through the formal channels, on purely technical grounds. They look askance at the idea of establishing good relationships with work colleagues other than those with whom they are in direct formal contact (such as members of their own team) or those who happen to share a common social or sporting interest. Networking for other reasons is seen as insincere: 'sucking up to the boss' is one of the more polite terms used for networking upwards.

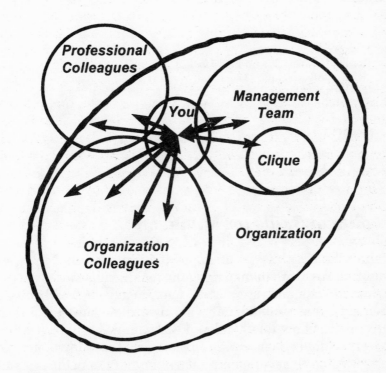

A simple network model

The facts of organizational life, however, do not support this simple viewpoint and limited style of managing. Few decisions on change are made purely through formal channels, or purely on technical grounds. Most managers need the support, information and resources that only a network can provide. And the manager without an understanding of the social element of networks and change is more likely to try to force through an unsuccessful project than the manager who is sufficiently sensitive to realize that more time must be spent discussing the matter, and gathering information and support, if the change is going to be effective.

Networks are important means of trade and mutual support. As an exercise, take a large sheet of paper and draw your network of relationships. Include the actual names of people in the network, rather than their job categories. Ask yourself: What information, support or resources can they provide for you? What can you provide for them? Are there relationships which are weakening, which you should strengthen? Are there people you would like to add to the network?

REFERENCES

Kanter, Rosabeth Moss, *The Change Masters*, Unwin, 1983.
Kaplan, R. E., and Mazique, M., *Trade Routes: The Manager's Network of Relationships*, Center for Creative Leadership, South Carolina, 1983.
Kotter, J., *The General Managers*, The Free Press, 1982.

See also model 47.

47. Political Skills for Managers

Managing the politics of a change situation can be of equal or greater importance than managing the technical issues – yet the political dimensions are often overlooked or deliberately ignored by some professionals, because they regard political activity as somehow unethical and distasteful.

Simon Baddeley and Kim James of the University of Birmingham have developed a matrix model to encourage and help professionals and managers in local government to overcome this reaction and to look on political skills in a more positive light.

The model maps an awareness of the political dimensions of issues against integrity to produce four categories: these can be seen as types of person, but it is more useful to see them as types of behaviour.

Fox	Owl
unprincipled, politically aware, self-seeking and politically skilled	principled and politically aware
Donkey	**Sheep**
unprincipled and politically unaware; self-seeking but reads the situation clumsily	principled and politically unaware, places a naïve trust in surface appearances and in the technical merits of a case

The model associates political awareness with an understanding of:

- formal processes and procedures;
- coalitions and the location of power and interest;
- the viewpoints of stakeholders;
- the grapevine and how to tap into current information;
- the need for support from others, and for negotiation.

Integrity is associated with:

- principled and ethical behaviour;
- being open and sharing information;
- loyalty and friendship.

The model presents all Sheep with a worthy alternative to the Fox – and indicates that an understanding of organizational politics does not necessarily entail a loss of integrity. And whereas all the other animals view issues as 'either . . . or', as winning or losing, the Owl looks for win-win situations.

Using the model
The dimensions of the model are helpful for analysing and discussing aspects of behaviour. In a number of cases where the model has been introduced to managers, we have seen it have exactly the effect that Baddeley and James intended – an

increased willingness to understand and work with the political elements of a situation, in a principled, problem-solving way. (Owl behaviour is very similar to assertive behaviour – see models 1 and 2.)

You can use the model to analyse your own behaviour and the behaviour of others. In the course of an average working day you may see examples of all four types of behaviour. As political awareness depends in part on an understanding of specific situations, whenever you move into a new area of activity you may find yourself behaving in more Sheep-like (or more Donkey-like) ways.

The four categories are, of course, rather blunt instruments with which to explore the delicate ethical issues which can arise in organizational politics – even allowing for qualifying adjectives (slightly Foxy, a little Owl-like, rather Sheepish, etc.), and you will probably benefit most from the model by using it to open up a personal exploration (or a discussion with others) of ethics and organizational understanding – and benefit least if you simply apply the four labels to the behaviour (or the people) that you meet.

REFERENCE
Baddeley, Simon, and James, Kim, 'Owl, Fox, Donkey or Sheep: Political Skills for Managers', *Management Education and Development*, Vol. 18, Part 1, 1987.

48. Stakeholder Analysis

Stakeholders are people who have an interest in a particular issue, and therefore may be inclined to influence any decisions that are taken about it.

When we attempt to bring about change in an area, or become involved in any issue, it is often useful to identify likely sources of support – stakeholders who might be allies – and opposition – stakeholders who might oppose us, or stakeholders with whom we may need to come to an agreement.

How we try to manage stakeholders will depend on their levels of power and interest.

There are a number of possible sources of *power* for stakeholders:

1. Position in the hierarchy: some stakeholders may be in senior positions, with formal authority covering resources which may affect the issue in question.
2. Purchasing power: customers who are affected by the issue may be in a position to influence the outcome.
3. Position in the process: the people who will implement a policy can have a significant effect on its success or failure.
4. Expertise: people with knowledge and skills about significant areas that affect the issue in question – such as technical specialist knowledge or knowledge of the market – may exercise a degree of influence.
5. Access to influence: which may come from personality or charisma, and the opportunity to influence people with formal power.

The level of *interest* of stakeholders in a particular issue is likely to depend on the extent to which the issue impacts the aims and assets of the stakeholders.

A matrix of power and interest can provide a guide on what may be the best approaches to take.

Stakeholders who are low in power and low in interest require little effort, whereas those who are low in power but high in interest can be kept informed of plans and progress.

Some stakeholders who are high in power may have little interest in the matter. One strategy for this group may be to attempt to raise their interest and enlist their support. Another approach is to attempt to identify their minimum concerns, and to make sure that your plans don't antagonize them and arouse their opposition.

	High		
	Keep checking		Main players
LEVEL OF POWER Medium			
	Not relevant		Inform
Low			
	Low	Medium	High

LEVEL OF INTEREST

Stakeholder Mapping Grid adapted from Mendelow, 1991, by Johnson and Scholes, 1997.

The key stakeholders are those with a high level of power and a high level of interest in the issue. As you are planning changes it is obviously important to align your plans, where possible, with what this group of stakeholders (or a sufficient number of them) considers acceptable. The main allies and opponents of contentious proposals will be found in this key grouping.

Using the model

Some managers' first experiments with this framework, as they attempt to identify the different categories of stakeholder, demonstrate difficulty in separating power and interest. In particular, they often overlook high power, low interest stakeholders.

If your first attempts produce similar results, step back from the issue a little. Are there stakeholders who could get involved, but at present are not active on the scene (because of lack of interest)? Could you recruit them as allies to your cause? And are all the powerful stakeholders you have identified really as interested in the issue as you think? Is there some way in which you can check out their level of interest?

REFERENCES

Johnson, Gerry, and Scholes, Kevan, *Exploring Corporate Strategy*, Prentice Hall, 1997 (4th edn).

Mendelow, A., 'Proceedings of 2nd International Conference on Information Systems', Cambridge MA, 1991.

Stakeholder analysis can be used alongside the other change models, such as models 41, 42 and 43.

Strategies and Structures

Strategic management is the endeavour of matching over a sustained period of time the capabilities of the organization with the requirements of the organization's markets and clients. It is characterized by a concern with the whole picture of the complex interactions between the organization and its environment, and between the different sections, sub-sections and interest groups within the organization. Strategic and operational management form the two parts of the organizational double loop (see model 20). Where operational management is concerned with the details of production and achievement in the short to middle term, strategic management should be concerned with the longer-term, wider-scale implications of activities.

Managers with a strategic brief, therefore, should look both outside and inside the organization, at:

- the position of the company in its various markets – its market shares, the actions of its competitors, and the broad environmental factors that may have an effect on its fortunes now and in the future;
- the resources – including the skills and competencies – which the company has at its disposal, and the way these are organized and developed through structures and systems.

For the first half of the twentieth century it was thought that enduring rules and principles of organizational structure could be discovered, which would apply in all circumstances. Since the 1960s, however, it has generally been accepted that a contingency approach should be adopted, and it is recognized that the shape of the most effective organizational structures, systems and cultures depends on a number of factors, particularly the rate of change in the environment, and the degree to which products and services can be standardized.

An understanding of key strategic models is vitally important for senior managers within organizations. These models provide structure and guidance on future action. Such an understanding is also important for managers in more junior positions, to help them to align their actions, their aims and their pr proposals with a realistic view of company strategy.

In working with managers at all levels, we have found the following models to be particularly useful:

49. Developing Strategy
50. Excellence Models
51. Winning Companies
52. Corporate Culture
53. Product Life Cycle
54. PEST Analysis
55. Competitive Strategy
56. The Marketing Mix
57. Configuration
58. The Learning Organization
59. Core Competencies
60. BCG and MCC Matrices
61. Downsizing

49. Developing Strategy

Early approaches to strategy used a model of long-range planning and emphasized rational analysis of all the factors that can affect an organization.

However, more recent models see successful strategy as the result of a series of incremental decisions in pursuit of a broad goal. Senior managers have a reasonably clear idea about the desired goal of the organization, but move towards this position step by step, solving problems and taking advantage of opportunities as they arise. Strategic decisions may emerge out of the debates between different stakeholders in the strategic process. This incremental approach is more likely to overcome the uncertainties of the future than an approach based on detailed long-term planning.

This model of how to formulate successful strategy is called *logical incrementalism*.

But incremental change may not always keep step with changes in the company's environment, and a more fundamental strategic change – a *transformational change* – may be necessary.

Incremental change in company strategy may fall behind the rate of change in the environment – often because of the culture, values and beliefs of the organization, which in some cases will cause managers to misinterpret strategic signals. (Of course, it is possible for a company to move too fast for the environment – for example, the problems of Apple in the 1990s of introducing too many technological improvements for the market.)

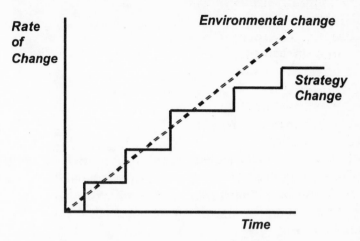

From Johnson and Scholes, 1997 (reproduced with permission).

In the case in the diagram above, the strategy of the company has moved incrementally in the right direction, but it is not moving fast enough to keep pace with environmental change. A strategic gap opens up, sales decline and the company goes through a period of turmoil and crisis. Out of this may come a transformational strategy, entailing much change, to reposition the company. Alternatively, the company may fail to overcome the strategic gap, and may go out of business.

Using the model
The first value of the model is to warn us against putting too much faith in the detailed long-term strategic plan as a means of effective strategy formulation. This does not mean abandoning positive strategy, but encourages us to identify goals, directions and processes for making the necessary incremental decisions on strategy. Paying attention to processes for discussing and making strategic decisions is very important if we are not to lurch from controversy to crisis to controversy with every attempt to develop the company strategy.

Secondly, we may hope to achieve successful strategic goals by incremental moves, lagging and leading the environme' changes by only small degrees – but a more likely pattern fo formulation of strategy, particularly given the unpredictable pace and nature of change, might be periods of incremental strategy that are interspersed with crises and the need for transformational changes.

REFERENCE
Johnson, G., and Scholes, K., *Exploring Corporate Strategy*, Prentice Hall, 1997 (4th edn).

50. Excellence Models

Tom Peters and Robert Waterman's influential *In Search of Excellence* studied 43 successful and innovative US companies. The companies characteristically emphasized quality, empowerment, good communication and the importance of company culture.

Peters and Waterman identified eight principles of excellence:

1. *Stick to the knitting.* Successful companies build on their core strengths and do not stray too far away from them.

2. *Close to the customer.* Successful companies strive to anticipate customer needs. Good communication with the customer is important, as is a positive company image.

3. *Autonomy and entrepreneurship.* Empower people and encourage them to take risks and innovate.

4. *Productivity through people.* Treat staff as responsible adults, with tough-minded respect. Train staff and set them reasonable and clear expectations. Avoid artificial and unnecessary divisions between management and staff.

5. *Hands-on, value-driven.* Create a strong, positive culture based on a clear set of principles, to provide a sense of shared direction. Promote the culture through the actions of management: encourage and model 'management by walking about' (MBWA).

6. *Bias for action.* Avoid 'paralysis by analysis' – encourage constant experimentation and expect to make progress by trial and error. Use task forces and 'adhocracy' to find quick solutions to problems.

7. *Simple form, lean staff.* Use simple organizational forms, and split into small units wherever possible. Avoid complex systems such the matrix organization form.

8. *Simultaneous loose-tight properties.* Encourage autonomy, fluid organizational forms and risk-taking (the loose), while at the same time require that short-term financial returns meet targets, and protect the core values (the tight).

Peters and Waterman related these principles to the basics of successful business – which they saw as:

- quick action;
- service to customers;
- practical innovation;
- the need for everyone's commitment in order to achieve the first three points.

The excellence model has had a tremendous impact on how the route to successful strategy is described, with its practical emphasis on customer perception, empowerment of staff and the importance of company culture. As Ralph Stacey has pointed out, Peters and Waterman's promotion of intuition, vision, culture and charismatic leadership was in tune with a reaction against the then-dominant view that success could be achieved solely through rational planning and control.

Each of the eight principles is discussed in more detail in *In Search of Excellence*, with examples from Peters and Waterman's research. The research – a strong selling point of the original model – delivered a number of hostages to fortune, as many of the companies Peters and Waterman cited as exemplars of good practice ran into trouble in the years that followed the publication of the book. Research in the UK in the early 1990s, however, resulted in a similar list of characteristics (see model 51).

Using the model
Identifying the eight attributes of successful companies is much easier than actually applying them to your own practice – particularly if they describe a state of affairs which is very different from current practice within your company.

Applying them within your company might mean:
- identifying core competencies and divesting in other areas (*Stick to the knitting*);
- improving all aspects of communications with the customer (*Close to the customer*);
- introducing and sustaining styles of management, systems and structures that encourage empowered action by staff (*Autonomy and entrepreneurship; Productivity through people*);
- developing a positive entrepreneurial culture (*Hands-on,*

value-driven; Bias for action);
- simplifying structures and targets (*Simple form, lean staff; Simultaneous loose-tight properties*).

A good starting point is to use the model as a checklist, to see how much change would be needed within your organization.

REFERENCES
Peters, T. J., and Waterman, R. H., *In Search of Excellence*, Harper and Row, 1982.

See also Stacey, Ralph D., *Strategic Management and Organisational Dynamics*, Pitman, 1993.

51. *Winning Companies*

Research carried out for the Department of Trade and Industry and the Confederation of British Industry by Warwick Business School identified a number of characteristics of successful UK companies which are similar to the 'excellence' characteristics of Peters and Waterman.

The research produced a model of these characteristics, together with case study examples of the characteristics in operation. According to the research, competitive – or 'winning' – companies:

1. *Are led by visionary, enthusiastic champions:*

- leaders have a vision that is owned throughout the organization;
- they build demanding but realistic targets into the business strategy;
- they are champions for change who lead by example and accept managed risk;
- they generate an open communicative management style throughout the organization.

2. *Know their customers:*

- have a realistic understanding of their competitors and how to beat them;

- know the drivers in the market;
- focus on the customer and cultivate an active partnership towards total customer satisfaction.

3. *Unlock the potential of their people:*

- empower all employees by creating individual ownership and focus on customers;
- simplify the internal systems wherever possible;
- clearly communicate company performance;
- encourage a team approach and train at all levels;
- benchmark performance against direct competitors and other companies.

4. *Deliver products and services that exceed their customers' expectations:*

- adopt a philosophy of total quality in all company behaviour that emphasizes delighting the customers with all aspects of the products and services;
- measure customer perceptions of products and services;
- continuously seek to reduce costs to the customer.

5. *Continuously introduce differentiated products and services:*

- have a product-and-service-after-next philosophy;
- exploit new technology or legislation to drive new product innovation;
- customize the product and service;
- deliver continuous improvements in all aspects of added value.

This is a visionary perspective on competitiveness that is based on what is evidently sound research, and supported by detailed illustrations. The model emphasizes empowering leadership, innovation and a strong market focus.

Using the model
The model can be used in the same way as the excellence model (model 50), as a framework for auditing and then improving your own organization. As its themes are complementary to the excellence model, it can be used as an explicit addition to Peters

and Waterman's work – and it is perhaps particularly suitable for use in this way with UK companies who may be able to relate more easily to its origins and to the more local case study examples than to the large corporations from which the American model was originally developed.

Questionnaires to identify current practice and possible innovations and developments can be built on the foundations of the characteristics identified in the model, and priorities for action can be established. The process of discussing and using the model in this way can raise awareness of these inspirational characteristics.

As with the excellence model itself – and other inspirational models – there is often a need to work particularly hard to go beyond espousing the theory, and putting it into practice.

REFERENCE
Competitiveness – how the best UK companies are winning, DTI/CBI, 1994; based on research into UK firms by Warwick Business School.

52. *Corporate Culture*

Organizational culture has been generally recognized as a strong contributor to success following the work of Peters and Waterman, which emphasized a positive culture as a unifying, energizing, controlling element of strategy.

According to Schein, culture is an interrelated set of 'basic assumptions and beliefs that are shared by members of an organization, that operate unconsciously and define in a basic, take-it-for-granted fashion an organization's view of itself and its environment'.

A shorthand for company culture is: 'The way we do things around here'.

Schein saw company culture existing at three levels:

1. In company practices and behaviours – including procedures, reward systems, status symbols and the myths and stories which are told within companies to illustrate and exemplify the way things are done.
2. In explicit statement of values and beliefs – both official and public and unofficial and private.

3. In the deeply held, often unconscious assumptions which are shared by people within the company.

With the increasingly high profile of company culture, many organizations have included explicit expressions of corporate values in their mission statements. There may be considerable discrepancies between these espoused values, however, and the actual values that make up the culture – which can be detected in the actions and words of the members of the company, and the systems and procedures it operates.

Different parts of a large organization may have different cultures. These may be departmental cultures, or sets of values that apply at different levels in the hierarchy. Professional groups within the organization will import some of the values of their profession.

Areas where culture can have a significant effect on the behaviour of a company include attitudes towards:

- *customers and quality:* attitudes may range from a high concern with customer choice and customer satisfaction, to regarding customers as a nuisance who don't really know what they want;
- *staff:* attitudes may range from giving staff autonomy within limits, to strictly directing and controlling them;
- *innovation:* attitudes range from encouraging experimentation and tolerating a certain amount of failure, to requiring people to reproduce what has been successful in the past;
- *colleagues:* the predominant attitudes may encourage individualism and competition, or co-operation and teamwork.

Using the model
Reflect on the culture of your organization: it will be visible in the words and actions of the individual members of the company – particularly the more senior and influential members – and in the systems and procedures. Consider in particular the culture and values regarding the four bullet-point areas above. Do not confuse the actual culture with the official statements of corporate values. These may represent what senior management would like the culture to become – or what they would like other people to think the culture is.

Compare your assessment of the actual culture of the organization with the corporate value statements. Where are the discrepancies? What has given rise to the discrepancies?

Note that cultures may be strong or weak, and that there may be a core'of values across an organization – or the culture may be fragmented and strongest within departments. If you have worked for a long time within the same organization or department it may be more difficult for you to identify the culture: you are likely to have internalized many of the assumptions and beliefs. It will be helpful to visit and compare notes with people in other organizations, to gain perspective on your own situation.

As a manager and a leader, consider what values you want to promote within your team/department/organization. How can you promote them consistently in actions and words?

If, for example, an expressed value is to 'focus on the customer and cultivate an active partnership towards total customer satisfaction' (see model 51), what specific actions can be taken to make progress in this direction? Consider how you can use key values as goal statements, and set SMART targets to move in the direction of the goals.

REFERENCES

Johnson, Gerry, and Scholes, Kevan, *Exploring Corporate Strategy*, Prentice Hall, 1997 (4th edn), Chs. 2 and 5.

Schein, E., *Organizational Culture and Leadership*, Jossey-Bass, 1985.

Semler, Ricardo, *Maverick*, Arrow, Random House 1993.

See also models 8, 31, 34, 50, 51 and 63.

53. Product Life Cycle

Some market analysts expect products (and services) to have life cycles.

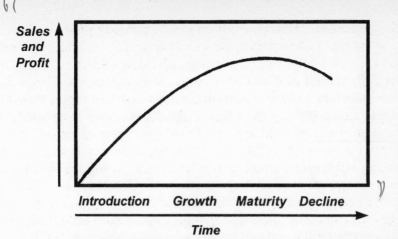

The financial marketing strategies for a product or service should vary according its stage in the cycle. For example, more investment or risk money is usually needed in the introduction and growth stages. At the introductory stage in the life cycle, the market will be very small and sales will be low. The company may need to invest heavily in order to develop the product, the means of production and the market.

If they are successful, the cycle will move into a period of growth. During this period, the company may continue investing in the product and improving production processes.

During the stages of maturity and decline, the company might sensibly use revenues from this product for other purposes – developing variations of the product to extend the life cycle, or investing in new products elsewhere. When the market for a product is judged to have reached maturity, many companies aim to introduce an improved variation, to attempt to boost sales.

Ichak Adizes views organizations as entities which have a similar life cycle:

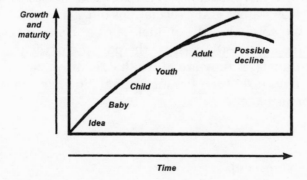

Adizes suggests there are typical problems at each stage, as a company grows and matures.

Using the model

Life cycles are useful models but, as with all strategic models, there can be certain difficulties about applying them in practice. For example, the length of the life cycle and the size of the market may be very difficult to estimate. Changes in technology and the scale of competition may lead to a much shorter life cycle than was originally predicted. On the other hand, established products and businesses may defy the move into decline: Coca Cola, both as a product and a company, has been at the mature phase of the cycle for many years.

Also, the patterns of growth, maturity and decline may not be as smooth as the diagram suggests. In the fashion and toy industries, a product may peak and fall several times.

However, these are just cautionary notes. This uncertainty will affect the movements of markets whether or not we use life cycle models as an attempt to analyse what is happening. The model provides useful descriptions of a series of stages which our product or service may undergo, and also offers us a warning that the situation may change from one stage to another.

As senior decision-makers, we might expect that we will have to support a new product with finance during the introductory stage – that we can't expect much return until some point during the growth stage. We might expect from the model that the growth rate will flatten out at some point as the market matures, and we can consider strategies for when that takes place. We might expect that at some point the market will decline. It can be useful to establish what stage the company has reached in its life cycle, and be ready to forestall or solve the more pressing of the problems that are likely to arise as the company grows – particularly by clarifying the roles, values and expectations of key players.

For a large company, the model can be used alongside the BCG grid (see model 60) to assess the position of the company's range of products. If they are all in the decline stage of the life cycle, it is obviously time for some dramatic action on the part of senior management.

REFERENCES
Adizes, Ichak, *Corporate Lifecycles*, Liber, 1991.

54. PEST Analysis

Organizations exist in broader systems and environments, and their successes and failures can often be related to environmental factors outside the organization.

PEST analysis is an established model for examining systematically these various factors, which are identified as:

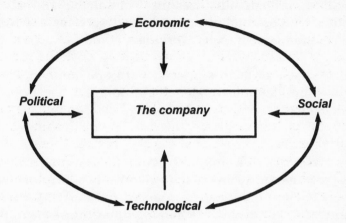

- *Political factors* – such as changes in legislation or regulations affecting company activities. This could include legislation regarding the goods and services the company provides, or terms and conditions regarding sale of goods and supply of services, or changes to legislation on health and safety, environmental protection, employment, trade union activity or discrimination. Political decisions may change tax levels. Local political factors may influence planning and use of land applications.
- *Economic factors.* The behaviour of the market is obviously a crucial factor for commercial organizations, where changes in the behaviour of customers and competitors can have an immediate effect on revenue. Changes in the economics of the factors of production – the price and availability of supplies and of workers with the necessary skills – will also affect company performance. Broader economic movements – such as levels of inflation and unemployment, the prevailing interest rate and international exchange rate – may have an impact on the behaviour of the markets.
- *Social factors.* Changing customs, expectations and patterns of behaviour may have effects on markets – increasing or

reducing the demand for products and services – and also on the way in which people inside the organization expect to relate to one another. In many markets, these social changes have a long-term, gradual effect, but changing demographics within an area can affect local markets within a short space of time.

• *Technological factors.* New products and services are made possible through advances in technology, and also new methods of producing products and services – which can have a dramatic effect on working methods.

The four sets of factors interact with one another. There are economic implications of significant political, social and technological changes.

Using the model
The model provides a simple structure for scanning for environmental changes, ensuring that no significant source of change is likely to be omitted. It can be used with the SWOT framework (see model 69) to consider emerging opportunities and threats. A typical use of PEST analysis is to consider probable changes in each of the factors over the next five-year period, and to assess the impact of such changes on the company. This may mean bringing together experts – or expert knowledge – in the four different areas. For many companies, the most significant influences will be specific economic and technological factors.

A company's environment may be relatively stable, with little change in the significant factors, or at the other extreme it may be particularly turbulent, with active competition, new entrants to the market, fluid customer demands and changes in available technology. In the latter case significant factors will require constant monitoring, with rapid feedback of the information to decision-makers within the company.

PEST is a broad framework, and each company will be able to identify specific factors which it should monitor – such as the actions of particular customers, competitors and suppliers, developments in crucial areas of technology, potential changes to items of legislation and so forth. You should be able to identify these for your company, as well as sources of information about each factor. How reliable and cost-effective are these sources of information? How often do you consult them?

On an occasional basis it is valuable to set aside the natural predominant bias towards short-term movements, and to consider possible scenarios in the longer term brought about by changes in any of the key factors. How might the company respond to these changes? What early indications might there be that the factors will change in this way?

55. Competitive Strategy

Michael Porter identified two generic competitive strategies. According to his model, companies can only compete in a market either on the basis of price or on the basis of differentiation.

If the products and services offered to a market by different companies are identical, customers will make their choices based on price. Choosing to compete on price is only sustainable in the long run if the company has a lower cost structure than its competitors – which may be achieved through capturing a significant proportion of the market and thus creating economies of scale – or is prepared to subsidize one product with revenues from another in the expectation of winning a long term advantage.

In many markets, companies aim to differentiate their products from those of their competitors, to enhance their appeal to the market. To this end, they introduce variations and improvements, and also create brand images to distinguish themselves from their competitors in the minds of their customers. Actual differences, or a strong brand image, can allow companies to charge premium prices. In some markets, despite strong branding activity, many customers still make purchase decisions on the basis of price and accessibility: the market for petrol or gasoline, for example, shows a high level of branding activity but is also very price-sensitive.

According to Porter, successful companies decide to compete either on price or on differentiation: they make a decision on their competitive strategy and stick to it. Johnson and Scholes, however, argue that some companies have successfully pursued a hybrid strategy of a mixture of price and differentiation – citing IKEA, the Swedish furniture and design company, and some Japanese car manufacturers, as examples.

The ability of a company to pursue a particular competitive strategy will partly depend on its market position. Michael

Porter's model of market structure identifies five significant factors that affect a company's position in the market:

1. the degree of active competition;
2. the threat of new competitors entering the market;
3. the availability of substitute products or services;
4. the bargaining power of buyers;
5. the bargaining power of suppliers.

Where the five factors are favourable (i.e. low levels of competition, low risk of new entrants, suppliers and buyers not powerful, low risk of substitutes), many companies can make profits.

Where competition with existing firms is fierce, a company may need to spend more money on differentiation, through marketing, promotion or product development, or there may be price competition, making the market less profitable.

In some markets there are high barriers to entry for new companies – such as the need to invest heavily in equipment, or to invest in acquiring or developing the necessary skills. High brand images of existing providers also act as a barrier to entry. These barriers can provide protection to firms in the market, and enable higher levels of profit to be achieved. Part of a company's competitive strategy can be to raise the height of these barriers – for example by achieving a high level of brand recognition, by developing key competencies and by mechanizing production processes.

In some markets, economic power lies at a particular point in the chain of production, from original producer to ultimate consumer. Companies at this point in the chain can dominate relationships with their suppliers or their buyers.

Using the models
Much of this analysis depends on understanding and defining the market. A first stage in using the models, therefore, is to identify your market and your competitors. Mass markets for manufactured products, such as personal computers, video cameras or televisions are relatively easy to identify. Larger mass markets may be segmented in bands of function and price (for example, computers, cars) and manufacturers' strategies may be to offer products to compete in each price band. For smaller companies, particularly providers of services, the

market may be more difficult to define.

The second stage is to identify the benefits you provide for the customers of your products or services.

A third stage is to identify your competitors, and any substitute products or services which customers may use. What differentiates your products and services from those of the competition? What are the price differences? Can you accentuate or develop differences in what you provide which will add value in the eyes of the customer?

REFERENCES
Johnson, Gerry, and Scholes, Kevan, *Exploring Corporate Strategy*, Prentice Hall, 1997 (4th edn).
Porter, Michael, *Competitive Advantage*, Collier Macmillan, London, 1985.

See also models 56, 59 and 60.

56. The Marketing Mix

The marketing mix is a well-known model of the characteristics of a product or service that, taken together, will affect its success or otherwise in the market. The marketing of a product is a manipulation of these characteristics to best match what customers want, relative to products and services offered by competitors, and thus to achieve the best results for the company. The direction and extent of the manipulation will depend on the market and the competition, but the model warns us not to focus all our efforts on one dimension of the mix without considering the others.

The four dimensions of the mix are:

* *Product/service design:* including the simple, tangible features of the core product, and the broader characteristics of the extended product. In a restaurant, for example, the core products are the food and drink, but the service and ambience are key characteristics for most customers – in some cases the other clientele and the reputation of the establishment are also important considerations. The significance of many design characteristics may be influenced by promotion activities.
* *Promotion:* includes a range of activities, from creating brand

images to publicizing them through advertising, merchandising displays and sales force activities. Sales may be encouraged by more publicity, and a larger advertising or selling budget – or by changing the image of a product and seeking a new market.

- *Price:* sales may be encouraged by reducing the price – but this may only succeed in reducing the company's overall income. The sales of some products are sensitive to variations in price, whereas others are less so. Price may be taken by the market as a reflection of quality, and a competitive strategy may be to increase the price along with taking action (through promotion, design and distribution) to influence the perception of product quality. Variations in price in the form of special offers may appeal to some parts of the market – such as early-evening happy hours in bars and restaurants, and discounted prices on public transport and in some hotels at times when the non-price-sensitive business users are not part of the market.

- *Place:* the distribution of the products and services, the access of the market to them, the location of the selling points may have a significant effect on sales. In the retail business, for example, location is an extremely significant factor affecting success. In some markets, competing companies use different place strategies, with implications for their cost structures and for the extended product they provide. In the home PC market, for example, some manufacturers sell through stores in the high street or shopping mall, whereas others sell only through direct mail order.

One suitable visual image of the mix is of the four faces of a pyramid, as each dimension represents a face of what the company is offering to the market. See from above:

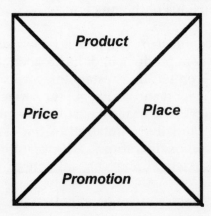

Using the model

You can use the model to analyse what your company is providing, in comparison to your competitors, and consider any changes that could be made in any of the four dimensions of the mix. In this way, the model can be used as a basic checklist for assessing your activities in marketing a product or a service.

As an exercise, for a product or service you provide, note what you are doing under each of the four Ps. Consider what is provided by your competition. Note any short-term, experimental actions you could undertake in each area to improve your competitive position. Beware also of any longer-term, more radical actions you could undertake in each area.

Note: There is, of course, a fifth face to a pyramid – the base. This can be taken to represent *market research*, your understanding of what your customers want, which provides an appropriate base to the four activities of the mix.

REFERENCE
McCarthy, E. Jerome, *Basic Marketing: A Managerial Approach*, Richard D. Irwin, Illinois, 1981.

See also model 55.

57. Configuration

Some key aspects of how an organization operates appear to be closely interconnected in certain configurations.

The best-known model of configuration is the 7S Framework designed for the McKinsey consultancy by Waterman, Peters and Phillips. The seven elements of the framework are:

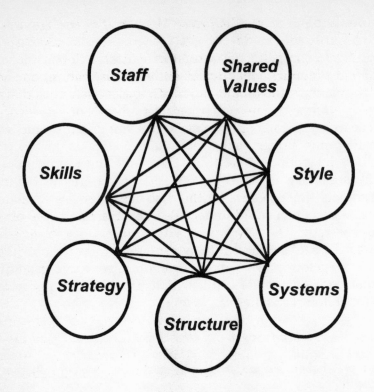

Strategy, structure and systems are the more tangible, hard elements: they are relatively easy for senior management to change. Style of management, staff, skills and shared values (or culture) are the less tangible, soft elements – equally important, but often more difficult to change in the direction that senior management desires.

All seven elements are interconnected and changes to one element may create changes (intended or accidental) in the others. Improved company performance is unlikely to come from changing one without attention to the others.

There is no single 'correct' configuration, but different combinations of the elements may be effective in different circumstances. Two broad types of configuration were identified by Burns and Stalker as *mechanistic* and *organic* types of organization.

- *Mechanistic configurations* contain many specialized, standardized jobs, in a hierarchical, graded structure. Job descriptions are detailed and specific. Co-ordination is carried out through the hierarchy, and most communication follows hierarchical channels. Mechanistic configurations will be most efficient in situations where there is little change, and they can gain the advantages of specialization.

* *Organic organizations* contain little specialization, and job definitions are loose and broad. Co-ordination is achieved largely through lateral discussions between colleagues. Organic configurations will be most effective where situations are subject to frequent change.

Using the model

The models remind us of the balance between different elements, and of the need to consider the broad potential effect of changes, rather than keeping a narrow focus on a specific area. Is the configuration appropriate for the current situation? If we aim to change one aspect of the configuration, what supporting changes will be necessary in the other elements? Or, what are the likely effects in the other elements?

For example, removing a layer of management (change to structure and staffing) will obviously require some changes to systems (of reporting, if nothing else) – but will probably also require changes in the skills of people who had been above and below the removed layer, and who are now in contact with one another, and probably some changes in the style of management. There is likely to be an effect, too, on the organizational culture: unless we take measures to influence culture in a positive way after removing the layer of management, it is likely to fragment or become negative.

This analysis seems reasonable and obvious – but the logic of it has not been followed by all the companies who have been anxious to downsize in the past ten years.

To take another example, a company may try to change its culture – but such an attempt is unlikely to be successful without supporting changes to the structure, systems and style of management (and perhaps also the skills of the people within the organization). A more empowered culture, for example, is not simply the result of a mass change of attitude (which management hope to bring about by training and development programmes, perhaps) but also of the delegation and transfer of more authority (structure and systems) and a greater degree of management trust and openness (style).

The configuration model emphasises the need for harmony, but complete harmony may be neither possible nor desirable.

Pascale has identified the need for both *fit* and *split* in organizational arrangements:

- *Fit* relates to harmony – but too much harmony can lead to the stagnation of conformity.
- *Split* relates to diversity, difference and possibly tension. Too much split leads to conflict and disintegration.

A balance over time of fit and split dimensions should enable organizations to experiment, innovate, change and consolidate.

REFERENCES
Burns, T., and Stalker, G. M., *The Management of Innovation*, Tavistock Publications, 1966.
Pascale, R. T., *Managing on the Edge: How Successful Companies Use Conflict to Stay Ahead*, Viking, Penguin, 1990.
Waterman, R., Peters, T., and Phillips, J., 'Structure is not organization', *Business Horizons*, June 1980.

For a broad introduction to issues of organizational design, see chapters 10 and 11 in Mullins, L., *Management and Organisational Behaviour*, Pitman, 1996 (4th edn).

58. The Learning Organization

The idea of a learning organization originates with Argyris and Schon's work on how organizations and their members react to change. In the simplest of terms, a learning organization may have either or both of these features:

- the systems of the company are designed to process information sufficiently well to avoid repeating errors, to adjust to new circumstances, and even to review fundamental policies and aims when this appears appropriate;
- the company provides an environment in which all its members are encouraged and assisted to learn new skills and perspectives, as required to help the company succeed.

The increased pace of change, allied with increasing competition, has highlighted the need for learning at all levels: for individuals to learn new skills; for decision-makers regularly to re-evaluate changing situations; for innovations in products, services and methods of working.

Peter Senge's vision of a learning organization is of a place where 'people continually expand their capacity to create the results they truly desire, where new and expansive patterns of thinking are nurtured, where collective aspiration is set free and where people are continually learning how to learn together'.

He identifies five 'disciplines', each of which he sees playing a vital part in building the learning organization:

1. systems thinking: to help us to understand the patterns and interrelations in events;
2. personal mastery: commitment to one's own lifelong learning;
3. mental models: developing more accurate models and visions of the world;
4. building shared vision: gaining commitment to an inspiring vision;
5. team learning: learning together in the 'fundamental learning unit' of the organization.

Another model has been produced by Pedler, Burgoyne and Boydell, who identified eleven characteristics of a learning organization.

Using the model
The idea of the learning organization is attractive to many people, combining a humanistic vision of co-operative working with the promise of more effective organizational performance. For these reasons, claims to be managing a learning organization have become fashionable, although the supporting evidence is often slight. Managers of extremely bureaucratic, inefficient and static organizations point to periodic reviews of systems and/or more training courses as proof they are running a learning organization.

1. *A learning approach to strategy*		2. *Participative policy making*	
The organization regularly evaluates and modifies direction and strategy as appropriate. Experiments are encouraged.		All members of the company contribute to policy making. Commitment to airing differences and working through conflicts.	

3. *Rich information flows*	4. *Supportive financial control*	5. *Customer concept*	6. *Reward flexibility*
Information and IT are used widely to help people understand what is going on.	Everyone responsible for managing their own resources. Finance people act as consultants and advisers.	Departments work to delight their internal and external customers. Managers facilitate rather than control.	Flexible working allows people to make different contributions and draw different rewards.

7. *Enabling structures*

Structures are seen as temporary, likely to change if required.

8. *Environmental scanning*	9. *Learning partnerships*
All staff are expected to bring back information on what is going on outside the organization. There are regular meetings with external customers and suppliers; there are systems for collecting information about the environment.	Work with other companies to share information and experiences – e.g. through placements, benchmarking.

10. *Learning climate*	11. *Self-development for all*
Attitude of continuous improvement. People keen to learn from events that have gone wrong, rather than blaming someone.	People have their own self-development budgets and are encouraged to develop their skills.

Based on Pedler, Burgoyne and Boydell, 1991.

It is perhaps helpful to consider learning organizations as a matter of degree: some companies will have many of the characteristics of a learning organization, others will have fewer. Improvement is a matter of progress up the scale.

To make genuine progress, a model such as that of Pedler, Burgoyne and Boydell can be used as the basis of a checklist for auditing the extent to which your company is a learning organization, and to identify priority areas for action. Senge's model provides a complementary approach, highlighting areas of skill and performance that can be enhanced to lead to the learning organization.

REFERENCES
Argyris, C., and Schon, D., *Organizational Learning*, Addison Wesley, 1978.
Pedler, M., Burgoyne, J., and Boydell, T., *The Learning Company*, McGraw Hill, 1991.
Senge, Peter, *The Fifth Discipline: The art and practice of the learning organization*, Century Business 1992.
Starkey, Ken, (ed.), *How Organizations Learn*, Thomson Business Press, 1996.

See also models 20, 34 and 63.

59. Core Competencies

Competency and competence approaches have become part of the language of management over the last ten years. There has been a concern with identifying and developing the competencies of individual leaders and managers. There has also been a growing concern with the competencies of an organization.

Gary Hamel and C. K. Prahalad originated the approach. They argue that the focus on products and markets followed by most strategic writers is misguided, as is a focus on a corporation's strategic business units. A company's products are like the fruit of the tree, according to Hamel and Prahalad. The roots – the main source of nourishment – are the core competencies of the corporation, and it should be an essential part of the strategic task of senior managers to identify and develop these core competencies.

Hamel and Prahalad see core competencies as:

- capabilities of an organization that represent a 'bundle of constituent skills and technologies' (Hamel and Heene, 1994). A core competency is likely to contribute to a range of end products or services. An accurate company analysis might identify between five and fifteen core competencies;
- capabilities that make a fundamental contribution to the customer's perception of the benefits of the end product;
- capabilities where the company has a comparative advantage over competitors.

Core competencies represent the collective learning within an organization, and typically comprise the co-ordination of a number of diverse production skills and technologies: for example, the way Casio brought together skills in miniaturization, microprocessor design, materials science, and thin precision casings to produce miniature calculators, digital watches and pocket TVs.

Some aspects of the care competency model appear similar to the old, traditional focus on production capabilities (as opposed to the more recent focus on the market). But a production capability is only a core competency if it helps to produce something the market wants. Hamel and Prahalad encourage both an analysis of the company's resources *and* an awareness of market needs as the key to sustainable strategy.

To build on core competencies, companies develop core products (the trunk of the tree) which can form components of final, end-user products (the fruit). A way of maintaining leadership in their chosen core competence areas is to become the leading producer of the relevant core products.

Hamel and Prahalad focus on technological, manufacturing competencies. Stalk, Evans and Shulman identified a number of company processes – such as Honda's capabilities in dealer management – which they thought were complementary to core competencies in providing competitive advantage. These are included as a type of competency – called 'functional process competencies' – by Thompson and Richardson, who identify thirty key corporate competencies in eight groups.

Using the model
Use the ideas within the model to identify the competencies of your company. The competencies may be technological or they may be to do with other aspects of corporate processes. You may be able to identify them by starting from why your customers value your products and services, and then working back through the skills and processes that enable you to provide these products and services.

Competencies are a combination of different skills, and if your first list is a long one it may be that it is a list of constituent skills.

From the list of competencies, identify those which are core to your company: they will be the competencies that make a significant contribution to those characteristics of the end product that are most valued by the customer, and the competencies where the company has a competitive advantage. Consider how to make best use of, protect and develop the core competencies – and make this consideration a key part of your strategic thinking.

REFERENCES

Hamel, Gary, and Heene, Aime (eds.), *Competence-Based Competition*, Wiley, Strategic Management Series, 1994.

Hamel, Gary, and Prahalad, C. K., *Competing for the Future*, Harvard Business School Press, Boston, 1994.

Hamel, Gary, and Prahalad, C. K., 'The Core Competence of the Corporation', *Harvard Business Review*, May/June 1990.

Stalk, George, Evans, Philip, and Shulman, Lawrence E., 'Competing on Capabilities: the New Rules of Corporate Strategy', *Harvard Business Review*, March/April 1992.

Thompson, John, and Richardson, Bill, 'Strategic and competitive success: towards a model of the comprehensively competent organization', *Management Decision*, 34/2, 1996.

See also model 60.

60. BCG and MCC Matrices

The Boston Consulting Group in the 1960s developed the Boston Matrix to analyse the market position of products and services. The matrix plots market growth against market share. Managers can use it as a starting point to review the strategic position of the company's products and services.

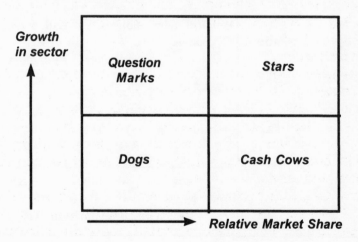

* *Stars* are those products where the market share and market growth are both high. The company may be a dominant force in this growing market. This is a key area for management's attention.
* *Question Marks* are those products where the market is growing, but the company's share is low: can they be moved

to Star status? Or is the company reconciled to having a small part of the market? Should it get out of the market altogether?

- *Dogs* are products with low market growth and low market share: unless they show signs of moving, the company should get rid of them.
- *Cash Cows* are those products where the market has stopped growing, but the company has a dominant market share. They can provide a source of income for other projects within the company.

The Boston Matrix is a well-established model. An alternative analysis has recently been produced by John Nicholls, who argues that strategic decisions about which projects to support should be related both to the company's mission, or strategic purpose, and its core competencies.

		Low	Medium	High
	High	Look for a joint venture	Develop by building the competence	Cherish
Fit with the mission	Medium	Watch closely; do not delay decision	Maintain, but not indefinitely	Allow pursuit by an 'intrapreneur'
	Low	Discard	Watch closely; do not delay decision	Separate into a subsidiary

Fit with core competencies

The Mission/Core Competencies (MCC) directional policy matrix
From Nicholls, 1995. Reproduced by permission of John Nicholls Associates (tel: 01832 733753).

Using the models
The BCG model can be used to analyse the range of products and services provided by a company, as a guide to formulating

strategy and investment decisions. As with the product life cycle (see model 53), a difficulty with using the model lies in knowing when the market has stopped growing: is a product a Star – worthy of further investment which will be repaid by continuing market growth? Or a Cash Cow – which should now be milked for all it is worth? The BCG terms are part of common parlance among marketing and strategic managers.

The MCC model has much wider potential application. It can be used to evaluate any project – not only those which are immediately linked to products and services. In tune with the core competencies approach to strategy, it can lead us to a level of analysis beyond the current performance of products in the market. It can also be used in the absence of hard information about a company's relative performance in the market place – information which is not available to many small and medium-sized enterprises, for whom the BCG is of limited relevance. It can also sharpen the debate within a company (or sharpen the analysis within an individual manager's mind) about exactly what core competencies the company possesses, and what it should be doing about developing them.

REFERENCES
Nicholls, John, 'The MCC decision matrix', Management Decision, Vol. 33, No. 6, 1995.

See also model 59.

61. Downsizing

A theme since the early 1980s in the USA has been that of competing through productivity – shedding fat to create a lean, fit, more productive company. In many cases this has meant examining how to shed jobs – with the benefit of a short-term saving in salary costs. Originally called 'downsizing', a recent variation of the term has been 'rightsizing' (although the right size is in fact almost always smaller). In the UK, 'restructuring' has been used to describe the process.

Downsizing has been achieved by changing working methods, reallocating responsibilities, using information technology in new ways and contracting out work that would have previously been done within the company. Contracting out takes the customer concept to its logical extreme: what was once a service provided by someone employed by the company is now supplied by another company, of whom the original company is in legal fact a customer.

The use of information technology has been a significant factor in the ability of many organizations to 'de-layer' strata of middle managers and achieve a flatter form. In some industries, more use has been made of temporary and part-time staff, in addition to a shrinking full-time core, to provide a more flexible workforce.

A number of other initiatives have been allied to downsizing – including flexible team working and empowerment (see model 34) and re-engineering. The latter, an approach to improving efficiency by examining the value added by each of the activities in the production process, was originally intended to eliminate waste and bureaucracy. A survey in 1994 of 600 managers in large Western corporations indicated that 69 per cent of US and 75 per cent of European companies were using re-engineering (Mumford and Hendricks, 1996). There now appears to be considerable doubt, however, about whether more than a small minority of companies who adopted re-engineering approaches made long-term gains in productivity.

Gary Hamel and C. K. Prahalad have criticized downsizing as being more to do with 'shoring up today's businesses than creating tomorrow's industries'. They agree that cutting back on fat is important to corporate health, but they are concerned that not enough senior managers understand the 'dividing line between cutting fat and cutting muscle'. Companies that strive to achieve the lean shape associated with good health may instead achieve only 'corporate anorexia'.

American economist Stephen Roach, formerly a leading proponent of 'productivity-led recovery', expressed a change in view in 1995. 'If you compete by building,' he wrote, 'you have a future. If you compete by cutting, you don't. If all you do is cut, then you will eventually be left with nothing' (*IoS*, 1996). In similar tones, the chief executive of PepsiCo says, 'You can't save your way to prosperity' (*IoS*, 1995).

Technological and economic pressures have led companies and public sector organizations to seek cost reductions and improvements in productivity. Improved productivity can be achieved by reducing resources (or the cost of resources) and producing the same amount of goods and services – and this is one of the routes to downsizing.

Another strategy to improve resource productivity has been to buy in services or functions that were previously performed in-house – the logic being that the company only pays for the service when it is required, and the providers of the service are not a continual item on the wages bill. However, the cost of buying back the service may be higher per unit required than the cost of producing a unit in-house. A number of redundant middle managers who have returned to their old employers as consultants have seen their incomes increase. In addition, there is a danger that the company loses valuable expertise by dispensing with experienced staff.

A different strategy to reduce costs is to cut back on resources, including selling off parts of the organization – which results in short-term gains in funds for shareholders.

An alternative strategy is to increase revenues by increasing the amount of goods and services produced by the same level of resources. This may mean innovating and producing different products or services to those the company currently provides, or moving into new markets with existing products. In the short term this is riskier than cut-back strategies. In the longer term, Hamel and Prahalad and other writers in this vein believe that innovation and expansion are the more likely route to success.

An additional risk of downsizing, indicated by Hamel and Prahalad, is that companies may actually dispose of activities which are their core competencies, their source of competitive edge. A more positive approach, the writers say, is to identify the core competencies and build upon them (see model 59).

Using the models
There are a number of mental models in operation in respect of downsizing, and job losses also raise emotional, political and ethical issues.

Models about the responsibilities of the organization to provide employment have changed in recent times. Most organizations and perhaps most employees have moved from a model of 'a job for life' (if they ever subscribed to it in the first place) to a model of a limited commitment on both sides, with individuals likely to have a number of different jobs in the course of their working lives. This has increased the importance of individual learning – we may each need to learn new skills to carry out these different jobs – and some organizations have replaced the 'job for life' promise with the offer of training and learning opportunities that can help the individual acquire transferable skills to make them more employable.

A common mental model among senior managers is that they are presented with no choice but to downsize – that the way forward is to cut costs and increase savings. This conservative view is challenged by Hamel and Prahalad and some of the other writers cited above. When faced with the pressure to reduce costs and improve productivity, senior managers might usefully consider whether: (a) they are cutting fat or cutting muscle; and (b) they could increase revenues instead.

REFERENCES

Hamel, Gary, and Prahalad, C. K., *Competing for the Future*, Harvard Business School Press, Boston, 1994.

Hammer, Michael, and Champy, James, *Re-engineering the Corporation*, Harper, 1993.

Mumford, Enid, and Hendricks, Rick, 'Business Process Re-engineering RIP', *People Management*, 2 May 1996.

Independent on Sunday, 10 December 1995.
Independent on Sunday, 12 May 1996.

Achieving Results

Most of the models in this book are in one way or another about achieving results. The personal effectiveness models are about achieving individual goals, but they can also be applied to collective ventures. The self-awareness and self-development models concern building a foundation within oneself for achieving results. The leading and managing models are about achieving results through other people, and the change models concern choosing new directions and persuading others to assist us to achieve new goals. The strategy models are ultimately concerned with large-scale corporate results, and establishing a firm base for achieving them.

In this final collection of models we introduce some ideas about achieving results through managing systems and operations. In these situations managers are charged with meeting the needs of customers or clients, and with doing so efficiently, with the best use of resources. This is a generic role of managers, found in varying forms in every industry where companies depend for their survival on revenues from customers, and in every public sector organization where purpose and revenue are in some way linked to the provision of services to a client group or the community at large. There is a need to understand how systems operate, how specific problems have arisen and how they can be solved. There is a need to use frameworks to analyse situations and to resolve problems, and there is a need to find trade-offs between competing and conflicting priorities.

There are some simple models in this area of achieving results. Do we adopt a marketing perspective, looking outwards, identifying market needs and working to satisfy them? Or a production perspective, focusing inwards on systems and methods of production and improvement? Or a selling perspective, which aims to convince customers that our products can meet their needs? Today's conventional advice is that the marketing perspective is the right model – but it is not always easy to discover what the market wants, particularly if you are an innovator. And businesses generally do not start with a blank sheet: they have certain finite skills, and other limited resources (see model 59). They soon reach a point where they have specific products or services to sell.

The management of large-scale operations and systems leads us to establish standards and targets and then to exercise management by exception – concentrating our problem-solving capabilities on those cases where the standard has not been achieved.

There have been many quality initiatives in recent years, initially influenced by the success of Japanese companies, and attempts to promote models of continuous improvement. Several of the models in this section concern quality and customers, and improving what we produce and how we produce it. There is a premium on analysis in the models in this section. There is also a recognition that, in an imperfect world, gains in one area will be paid for by losses in another, and that our best expectation is to find the point of optimum balance, where the net gains and losses are most in our favour.

The models in this section can be used in conjunction with other models in this book. To manage the operational systems, we often need to convince, persuade and win the commitment of other people – areas that relate to the models in the section on leading and managing. As we identify solutions to problems, and need to trade off conflicting objectives, the change models become more relevant. The ways in which we manage and develop our self have obvious implications for how we manage events around us. And today's event can often only be fully understood in the longer-term contexts set out in the section on strategies and structures.

62. Links with Customers
63. The Customer Concept
64. Achieving Quality
65. Trade-Offs
66. Project Management
67. Systems Modelling
68. Fishbone Analysis
69. SWOT Analysis
70. Failure and Prevention Costs

62. *Links with Customers*

Closeness to customers is regularly associated with success (see models 50 and 51). If we are not linking well with customers it is difficult to understand and to meet their changing needs.

We can use a well-established model of supply channels to map our links with our customers, assess how close to them we are, and plan how we should manage the links. We may have immediate customers and also end-users. Here are examples of different supply chains from a producer to an end-user.

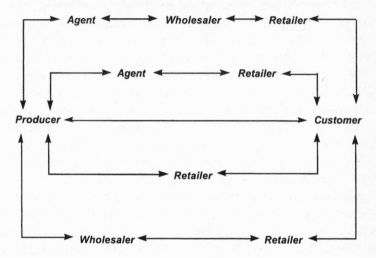

The model shows the links are two-way. Suppliers should encourage feedback on what is supplied.

A question for the producer is the net value of the intermediate customers. There is a trend in some sectors for producers to deal directly with customers, for example in insurance and financial services, and even in the UK car industry, where Daewoo are pioneering direct sales. The benefits of direct contact include:

- lower costs through cutting out commissions and intermediary mark-ups;
- better communication with the end-user.

However, the best channels of distribution will depend to a great extent on the type of business, and contact with an end-user may take more than one channel. For example, a producer of nuts and bolts may supply wholesale distributors. The producer will want the link with the wholesaler to cover stocking levels, packaging, etc., i.e. information on what the end-users are actually ordering. The producer may also want direct access to some classes of end-users – say, roofing companies who use the nuts and bolts in construction work. The producer may want a link with end-users to gather information on end-user satisfaction levels, product life in the field, etc.

Another model of links looks like this:

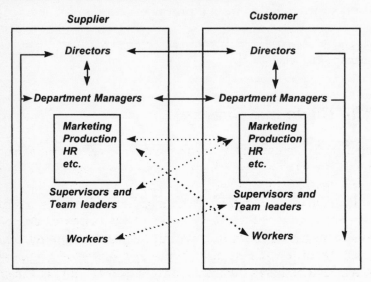

Typically, directors will meet with directors and managers will meet with managers. More organizations these days encourage links at other levels, aiming to cut out the usual hierarchical flow up one side, across, and down the other. For example, some companies encourage their operators to place orders and communicate directly with their counterparts in the supplying company when dealing with day-to-day problems.

Using the models
It is a useful exercise to map the links between you and your customers:

- Who are your immediate customers?
- Who are the customers of your immediate customers, the end-users?
- What benefit does each of the links in the chains add to the end-user satisfaction?
- What does each of the links in the chains add to your understanding of the end-users' satisfaction and the value placed on your product or service?

- If you have more than one chain, or several ways of linking to the customer or end-user, how can the channel be improved?
- How, and to what purpose, can better links be fostered throughout your organization with staff and workers at various levels in other organizations?

REFERENCES
See also models 63 and 67.

63. The Customer Concept

The customer concept is a model that has transformed many organizations in the past fifteen years – and transformed the espoused theory and terminology in many, many more.

Within large organizations, many employees are often remote from the ultimate customer. As one of our clients, the production manager of a traditional engineering company, once remarked: 'People used to think there was only one guy in the whole works who had a customer, and he was the guy at the end of the production chain.' This remoteness can breed carelessness about the quality of the work that is produced, and laxity about adherence to agreed schedules.

The customer concept is an attempt to

- improve the quality of work which is undertaken within a company;
- improve the value that is added to the goods and services the company provides to its ultimate customers;
- change the nature of the relationships between the people within the company.

The customer concept sees every worker and every team, section and department as a producer of services or products for customers internal or external to the organization. As the traditional engineering company moves to embrace the customer concept, the team at the first stage of manufacturing becomes the customer of the purchasing and the stores departments; the team at the second stage of manufacturing becomes the customer of the first-stage team, and so on. Each stage in the production chain is regarded as a relationship between customers and suppliers. And staff departments – such as personnel, IT and finance – becomes suppliers of services to their line manager customers.

Where the customer concept is applied, suppliers are encouraged to

- seek feedback from their customers about their level of satisfaction, and about whether they can recommend improvements to the service they receive;
- take more responsibility for quality and efficiency;
- work to improve their services and products.

Suppliers may be required to justify their jobs or their departmental budgets by virtue of the extent to which they meet their customers' needs. Staff departments may need to become more proactive, to develop and market services that line managers value and need.

Customers are encouraged to express their wants and register their feedback. Depending on the limits of the scheme, they may be given the freedom to buy services elsewhere if they are dissatisfied with internal suppliers.

Using the model
The customer concept benefits in its application from firm rules and definitions and clear sanctions. In companies where its introduction is a failure, the terminology – driven by senior management – may become part of the common language and a frequent topic for discussion, but, like the learning organization, the necessary measures required to ensure its implementation are lacking.

To implement the customer concept it is essential to have consistency and clarity in identifying who is your customer and exactly what products and services you supply. This may not be easy – you must start with the main products and services, including information, and work out from there. The situation – and the answers to these questions – may change, as it does for whole companies, and you may need regularly to review the position. Failure to achieve clarity at this point is fatal to implementing the customer concept.

Secondly, try to achieve clarity about customer and supplier roles. Confusion abounds, and the system becomes unworkable, where every communication is regarded as a product, and every recipient of that product a customer. Some communications will be from a customer to a supplier. In the interests of good practice, they should be clear, accurate and helpful – but they are not products supplied to a customer.

For example, take the staff appraisals I carry out on members of my team, and the report I produce: it is in practice not helpful to see this as a service I (supplier) perform for the team member (customer). It is probably more in the nature of the general flow of the relationship that I (representing the company) am a customer of the services the members of the team provide, and at the same time I have a responsibility to the company as a whole to develop and supply skilled and motivated workers. Much confusion can be avoided if it is accepted that customers have a responsibility to make their needs known to their suppliers.

Finally, mechanisms for discussing requirements must be created and the system must be given teeth. It may not be appropriate to allow internal customers the same sanction as external customers – the ultimate right to buy services elsewhere. This may be possible for some support services (transport, training, printing, catering, etc.) but is not likely to be practical for relationships along the production chain. Without some sanction, however, there is a danger that the customer concept will be no more than a thing of rhetoric and lip service.

You can progress the idea of the customer concept by considering questions such as:

- What products and services do you (in your team or section) provide?
- Who are your customers?
- What do they think of your services and products?
- Can you improve your communication with your customers?

- What products/services do you use?
- Who are your suppliers?
- What do you think of their products/services?
- Can you improve your communication with your suppliers and influence them to improve the services/products they provide?

64. Achieving Quality

For many years quality has been taken to mean the characteristics of a product or service which are valued by the customer.

Manufactured consumer products, for example – even simple ones – have a number of key characteristics that are valued by their purchasers, apart from their immediately observable features. Products which are used in a physical way (such as a belt, a propelling pencil, a saucepan, a pair of socks, a wristwatch) will be expected to have certain characteristics of functionality and durability – although exactly how effective, efficient or long-lasting they are expected to be will depend partly on the manufacturer's claims and partly on the price charged for them.

Ensuring these products reliably display these characteristics is a matter of quality management.

A quality management system consists of a number of interrelated components.

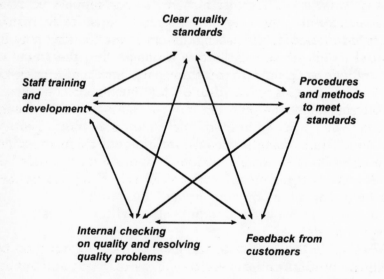

- *Clear quality standards* – product and service design activities should establish these, based on what customers expect, and they should then be communicated to everyone who has a hand in supplying the products and services.
- *Procedures and methods* – ways of working should be devised that will produce the goods to the required standards.

- *Staff training and development* – developing the necessary knowledge, skills and attitudes to enable staff to meet the standards.
- *Internal checking* – sampling, weighing, measuring, inspecting the goods to see if they meet the standards, observing work practices and procedures, and tracing and rectifying the causes of any quality problems.
- *Feedback from customers* – gathering information and reaction from customers to identify areas where expectations have been met, where they have not been met, and where they have changed.

The model has been developed from the manufacturing industry, but can be translated readily to many services. A number of hotels and fast-food chains, for example, aim to provide a service at all their outlets where the products and the approach to the customer have certain reliable characteristics – and this is achieved through the same five quality components.

In the context of continuous improvement, there should be constant activity in each of the five component areas. New customer expectations may be registered, new characteristics may be introduced, new procedures and new training may be required, and so on. In some markets the pressures of competitiveness have led companies to extend and enhance their idea of quality: avoiding quality failures – where characteristics of the product fail to meet basic customer requirements – is a limited aspect of achieving quality. Providing improvements and innovations which increase the value of the product to the customer, and not only satisfy but also delight, is the current extension of achieving quality (see model 51).

Using the model
You can apply the quality model to your own organization by taking any product and/or service you provide and noting how each of the five points applies.

A simple two-column approach to this exercise would identify:

- what you are doing now;
- what could be improved.

If you have the opportunity, contrast what you are doing with practices within a comparable company.

As an obvious extension of this exercise, consider what the customer reaction might be to a change in a key characteristic of the product or service – either to improve its quality or to improve your operational efficiency.

REFERENCES

The European Foundation for Quality Management has developed a corporate model for total quality within an organization: for more details contact EFQM, Avenue des Pleiades 19, 1200 Brussels, Belgium.

See also models 63 and 70.

65. Trade-Offs

Management is largely about making decisions. If everything ran itself, and sorted itself out when there were problems, no decisions would be needed. Decisions are necessary when there is a real choice between competing options.

Managers have many areas of choice. Often, making a decision in favour of one choice will have some negative impact on another. We may have to trade off the benefit on the one hand with a degree of loss on the other. For example:

• need to make the best use of resources	v	need to keep the customer satisfied
• back room	v	front room
• consolidation	v	growth
• training time	v	work time
• price	v	market share and volume
• convergent thinking	v	divergent thinking
• centralization	v	decentralization
• small and mobile	v	large and powerful
• stability	v	flexibility
• consensus	v	conflict and creativity
• product development	v	market development

In essence, the model of trade-offs is very simple, indicating that we have to balance competing demands. For example:

- *Back room/front room:* this is a well-known way of looking at organization systems. Organizations have people who look outwards, perhaps selling or dealing with customers. Behind them, seemingly locked away in the back room, are all the people who actually make the goods to sell. The tension typically arises when the front room bring in a big order that the back room have difficulty meeting. Or if a customer wants a particular colour for an item, which will cost the back room considerable time in resetting the paint machines. These tensions are also seen in the trade-off between *need to make the best use of resources* and *need to keep the customer satisfied*; *product development* and *market development*; and others.
- *Centralization/decentralization:* centralization supposedly leads to economies of scale, uniformity, consistency and control, with decisions being made at the top (at the centre). Decentralization supposedly leads to decisions being made closer to the action, more flexibility and initiative, with loss of direct control from the centre. A topical example is the continuing battle between computer departments with a preference for a central mainframe computer and dumb terminals on users' desks, where all software and systems are prescribed for the user, and end-users with a stand-alone PC, networked to share information but with their own programs and data storage.
- *Consensus/conflict and creativity:* consensus is obviously beneficial for mutual support, but an overemphasis on consensus may mean that people become afraid or unwilling to question accepted ideas and approaches. Individuality can give rise to innovation and experiment, but too much of an emphasis on individuality can give rise to competition and conflict that can destabilize the company. (See 'fit and split' in model 57.)
- *Training time/work time:* making time for training and development is likely to be of benefit in the longer term, as people learn the skills and knowledge they need for current and future success, but time spent on training and learning is time lost to producing today's results. Without good results today, the future of the company – and the individual's career prospects – may be bleak, and so there is pressure to produce short-term success, but companies run the risk of failure unless they also make provision for the longer term. (See model 38.)

Using the model
These trade-offs may be resolved at certain points in time – for example through systems that bring together the parties in the back room and the front room, or through systems that make achievement of training targets an important current result.

Consider your arrangements in each of the areas listed and identify trade-offs. When you are making changes, identify not only the gains but also the losses. Consider how you can best resolve the tension and achieve the most effective trade-off. Be alert to common ground, and to opportunities to achieve 'both . . . and' rather than just 'either . . . or'.

REFERENCES
Quinn, R., et al., *Becoming a Master Manager*, Wiley, 1990 (for a useful exposition of competing values).
Trompenaars, Lars, 'Developing the International Manager Strategically', in Garratt, Bob (ed.), *Developing Strategic Thought*, McGraw Hill, 1995 (for more examples of tensions and trade-offs).

See also models 44, 66 and 70.

66. Project Management

A project is a set of related tasks that has to be done to a defined standard, to a deadline, and with a defined amount of resources. Pressure on time and resources often creates a tension between these three factors.

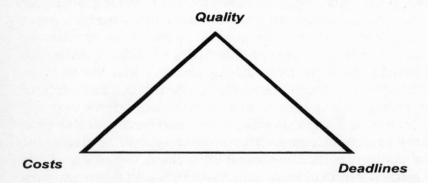

- *Quality – performance standards and measures:* these will vary according to the specific type of project. Some are likely to be essential and others desirable. At least some of the standards will be easily measurable, but others may be qualitative, the subject of judgement and opinion.

- *Costs of resources:* each project has resource requirements – measured in terms of financial, human knowledge/skills and materials/equipment needs. Ultimately all resources can be expressed in financial terms.
- *Deadlines:* the end-date for completion of the whole project, and perhaps any intermediate milestones.

Using the model

As a project progresses, there may be times when not all the requirements can be met, and you need to consider your priorities and possible trade-offs. At any point in time, one of the three points of the triangle may be dominant. For example, suppose a problem has arisen and *resources* are a serious constraint: no more resources are available. No more people, no more money, no more equipment or materials. You may need to consider reducing the quality of what you are producing, or extending the deadline, or even postponing or cancelling the project.

If *quality* is the critical characteristic – for example, where safety cannot be compromised – then solutions to problems may lie in increasing costs, or in extending deadlines. In other situations, where the *deadline* becomes critical, then quality may suffer or extra resources may be needed.

The issue for project managers is how to manage the competing requirements of each point, and, once the critical point is properly identified, how to negotiate with more senior managers or customers to redefine one or both of the other points.

In preparation for this, you need to have a clear specification of each of the three points of the triangle – and the extent to which there may be room for movement in the event of problems. For performance quality, try to identify the essential and the desirable characteristics. For resources, establish clear costs, and identify any critical resources – for example, the availability of particular equipment, or the skills and knowledge of particular individuals – which will be essential to the success of the project. For deadlines, work out a schedule of milestone dates when key stages of the project must be completed.

Most projects will involve a series of related tasks. The project schedule can be mapped with a Gantt chart (below) or a network diagram, either manually or by using a computer software product. The chart will show when linked tasks should begin and end in order to achieve the overall schedule. It can also be used to show resource requirements at each stage, and as a planning and control tool.

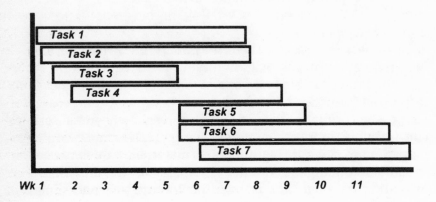

REFERENCES
Briner, W., Hastings, C., and Geddes, M., *Project Management*, Gower, 1996.

See also models 8 and 65.

67. Systems Modelling

Systems and processes can be modelled using simple line diagrams, showing sequences of activities. This can be effective in creating a snapshot of, for example, production systems. It may show unnecessary duplication of activities, or that certain activities are omitted, or performed at the wrong place in the sequence. In the example below, is it necessary to issue two order numbers, with the attendant paperwork, to components required for manufacture? And does the first inspection of them really not take place until after they have been incorporated in the manufactured product?

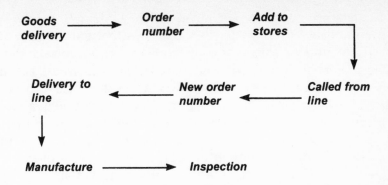

Line diagrams can represent control loops, or correctional loops, in a system. In the example below, the typical quality control loop is represented: samples of output are measured against a predetermined standard and, where necessary, information is forwarded to a point where someone can take corrective action – to identify the causes of any variations between the actual output and the standard, and to remedy the problem. In assessing the effectiveness of a system designed in this way, we might question how long each process takes. Can the sample be checked more quickly or closer to the point of manufacture? How fast can information about variations be forwarded? How quickly can corrective action be taken? Speed in this case is likely to be important: the longer the delay in any of these processes, the greater the amount of wasted output while problems continue to affect quality, unchecked and unresolved.

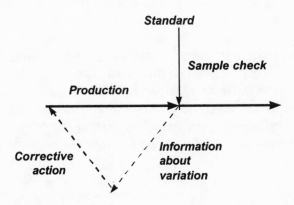

These are created systems within an organization, but line diagrams and feedback loops can also be used to map cause and effect in larger systems. The diagram below shows combined positive and negative feedback loops. Positive feedback loops build up an effect – they create virtuous or vicious spirals: Peter Senge represents them with the image of a snowball rolling down a hill. In this case a company innovates, and achieves success in the market place, leading to more revenue available for more innovation. There is also a negative, or correctional feedback loop here, however: seeing the success of the innovative company, competitors enter the market with me-too products, and this reduces the innovator's market success and revenues.

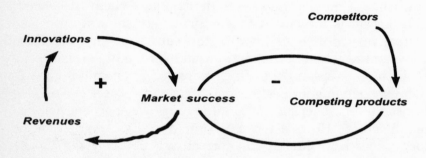

Using the models

This method of identifying and analysing the way systems work can be applied to a wide range of activities. Positive and negative feedback loops are common – separately and in combinations such as the one above. The examples here are about manufacturing, marketing and flows of finance, but personal reactions can be mapped in this way, too. Consider the positive feedback loop that exists between a person's self-confidence and their performance: more self-confidence leads to better performance, which can lead to more self-confidence.

REFERENCES
For further examples and extensions, see Senge, Peter, *The Fifth Discipline*, Century Business, 1992.

See also model 68.

68. Fishbone Analysis

Fishbone analysis is a systematic model for analysing and solving problems. It helps to separate the cause of a problem from the symptoms, and so can help us to avoid focusing only on the symptoms, or taking action which not does not solve the real, underlying problem, but causes new ones.

Fishbone analysis has been used widely for examining quality issues in manufacturing. It discourages jumping to the obvious (but possibly erroneous) conclusion, and can help us to identify multiple contributory causes of performance problems.

In this example, the apparent problem – job stress – is treated as a symptom, and the fishbone is developed to identify possible causes.

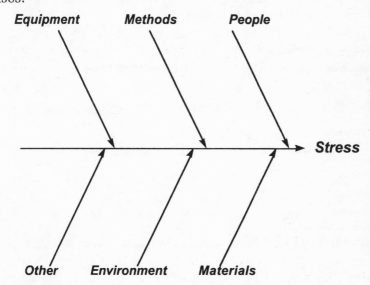

Using the model
Fishbone analysis can be used for solitary problem-solving or for tackling problems in a team.

In either case, it helps to be clear at the outset about the extent of the apparent problem, or symptoms, and to ask these questions:

- What are the features (symptoms) of the problem?
- Who is affected or involved? Who is not, but could have been?
- Which machine/system/business unit has the problem?
- When did it first happen?

So, for example, the apparent problem might be a high incidence of stress-related absences and below-average performances in a certain administrative team, affecting four members in particular, beginning prior to last Christmas.

Then consider the possible causes. It is often helpful to list the different main characteristics of possible causes as the main bones: as in this diagram, these may be *people, equipment, methods, environment* and *materials*.

If this is a team exercise, possible causes may be identified through brainstorming activities. Then, after a cooling-off period, the most likely possibilities can be marked for further investigation. For solitary problem-solving a similar principle can apply: think broadly and creatively about possible causes, then more logically and analytically about the most likely of the possibilities you have identified.

Some of the items identified as possibilities may appear far-fetched on mature reflection, whereas others may turn out to be major or contributory causes of the problem.

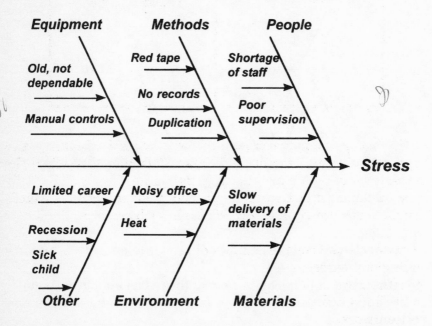

REFERENCE
Senge, Peter, *The Fifth Discipline*, Century Business, 1992.

69. SWOT Analysis

SWOT analysis is a systematic way of setting out information for planning and decision-making. It can be used at a strategic level for a whole organization; when considering the position of an individual product, service or project; or when evaluating the prospects of a department or section within a company. It can even be used to assess the position of an individual person – for career planning or staff development purposes.

SWOT stands for:

Strengths	*Weaknesses*
Opportunities	*Threats*

Strengths and weaknesses are internal factors, and opportunities and threats are external factors that affect the situation – or which may do so in the future.

When analysing a single department, for example, a SWOT might cover strengths and weaknesses such as:

- products and services supplied;
- responsiveness;
- efficiency;
- staff and skills;
- teamwork.

It might cover opportunities and threats such as:

- links with other functions;
- corporate plans;

- representation at strategic levels;
- links with the core business.

For a single product, we might consider SWOT factors such as:

- product design – features and functions;
- pricing, promotion and distribution factors;
- costs and profit margins;
- size of market and rate of growth/decline;
- share of market;
- actions of competitors;
- changes in technology or legislation affecting the market.

Using the model
Much of the value of SWOT lies in its use as a discussion tool to surface information and opinions and, through investigation and discussion, establish a degree of consensus about the true state of affairs as a preliminary to planning. After a thorough analysis has been undertaken, what can we do to make the most of the strengths and opportunities, develop the weaknesses and minimize the threats?

SWOT is often used as a format for capturing the information from group brainstorming. There are advantages in this, but there are also limitations.

To make best use of SWOT analysis it is important to spend time developing and refining any products of brainstorming. The size of the lists that emerge should be reduced by grouping and prioritizing, and clear and precise ideas should be developed about the meaning of factors. For example, in looking at the position of a section within an organization, someone may have suggested the 'skills of the staff' as a strength. This is too vague to be of value in further analysis. What skills are a strength? It is not necessary to reach the level of detail of a person specification, but we need to have more clarity about the nature of the skills. Are they functional/technical skills? Customer responsiveness skills? Team-working skills? On further investigation, some skill areas may be strengths, others may be weaknesses.

In using SWOT, it is also important to verify suggestions. As with fishbone analysis, which also lends itself to group discussion and brainstorming, the points put forward in an initial meeting usually repay further investigation. A noted threat may be the perception that a lower priced competitive product has entered the market: what can be done to verify that this is happening? Will the product appeal to some or all of our customers?

There may be disagreements about strengths, weaknesses, opportunities and threats – and if the analysis is to bear fruit these may require exploration and discussion. A thorough analysis is likely to be time-consuming.

Priority areas for action should emerge from SWOT – if the analysis has been sufficiently focused and clear, and based on sound, verified information.

REFERENCES
Hill, T., and Westbrook, R., 'SWOT Analysis: It's Time for Product Recall', *Long Range Planning*, Vol. 30, No. 1, 1997.
Stumpf, S. A., and Mullen, T. P., *Taking Charge*, Prentice Hall, 1992.

See also models 12, 54, 56 and 68.

70. Failure and Prevention Costs

There are a number of areas of operations where managers balance the costs of failure or breakdown and the costs of preventing failures.

This is obvious in the area of quality. Failure costs here are wasted time and materials, the costs of correcting internal failure and the costs of correcting external failure – providing replacement products or refunds and possibly compensation to dissatisfied customers. The prevention costs include the finance to pay for inspection, training and instruction.

It is also an equation in the management of stocks and supplies. Failure costs are measured in the expense of idle time for operators and machines, the costs of disruption, and lost sales (particularly in a retail context). The prevention costs are those of stock holding, inspection and management.

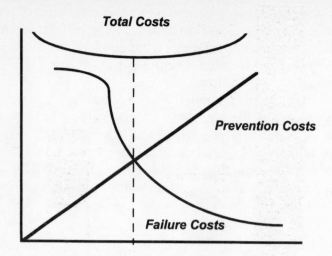

These calculations can also apply to issues of managing people. The costs of failure are those associated with poor performance and disciplinary incidents, and with the expenses of disruption and management time, whereas prevention costs are to provide time for effective recruitment, training, instruction, supervision and appraisal.

In the area of sales and marketing, the launch of a new product or service may entail considerable expense – on which there may be no return: prevention costs could include market surveys and product tests to estimate the possible attraction of our proposal.

Risk is a factor in assessing failure and prevention costs. Failure costs are often no more than possibilities: and only in large manufacturing or service operations – by virtue of their size – can the possibility be converted into a realistic percentage chance. Prevention costs, however, are usually real, here-and-now expenditures. And there is seldom a guarantee that they will completely prevent failure. In the examples above, expenditure on prevention should reduce the costs of failure in quality, stock management, people management and marketing, but may not eliminate failure costs altogether. This balance of certainty and risk is perhaps responsible for managers underspending on prevention in some areas.

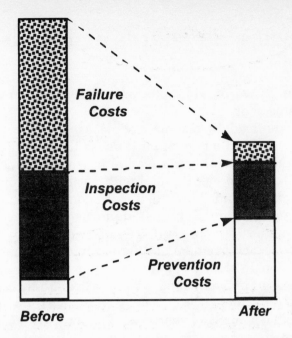

Using the model
In any chosen area of activity, consider the failure and prevention costs. Where it is possible to do so, calculate them in pure financial terms (this may help you to make a more compelling case for change). Consider whether enough is being spent on prevention – or too much is being risked in the area of possible failure. In many areas, a reasonable approach is to *increase* prevention costs, with the result of a *decrease* in inspection and failure costs.

Projects, Standards and Models

In this chapter we provide alternative ways of accessing the models in this book.

We have noticed that some people seem quite happy to identify the models that are of most use to them on the basis of the title of the model, or of the section in which it is contained. Other people are more concerned with particular projects they are undertaking, and how they can complete them more effectively or more quickly. It is quite natural for managers, habitually under pressure to produce results, to be more concerned with achievement of different types of project goals.

In the first part of this chapter we have listed some of the different types of project which managers commonly undertake, and indicated the models in this book which we think will be of most use in that context. Note that we do not by any means claim that these models are sufficient for effective completion of the project – you may need to apply many other ideas and techniques – but they will make a contribution to success.

In the second part of the chapter, we link the models to the Management Standards published in the UK by the Management Charter Initiative. The standards have been developed with the support of the Department for Education and Employment, and are the basis of many programmes and systems to develop managers. We list which models seem particularly relevant to which standards.

Capital investment	53 Product Life Cycle
	55 Competitive Strategy
Assessing whether to invest money in the expectation of future returns	60 BCG and MCC Matrices

Change	41–48 Change models
	1 Assertive Behaviour
Designing, evaluating and implementing any change within the organization	8 SMART
	9 Time Management
	13 Creativity
	69 SWOT
	52 Corporate Culture

Increasing competitiveness

Improving the company's
ability to meet customers'
needs more effectively and
efficiently than other firms

50 Excellence Models
51 Winning Companies
55 Competitive Strategy
56 The Marketing Mix
59 Core Competencies
63 The Customer Concept

Discipline

Assessing disciplinary issues
raised by staff

40 Modifying Behaviour
29 Motivation – the Process
30 What Motivates People?
19 Motivation to Learn

Distribution

Deciding on outlets and
transportation for the
company's goods and services

62 Links with Customers
56 The Marketing Mix
67 Systems Modelling

Downsizing

Reducing staffing through
redundancy to achieve
increased productivity

61 Downsizing
41–48 Change models

Empowerment

Encouraging staff to take more
initiatives and ensuring more
responsibility is exercised at
lower levels of the company

34 Flexible and Self-Managed
    Teams
51 Winning Companies
50 Excellence Models
31–33 Motivation models

Expansion

Increasing the scale of operations
and the size of the organization

60 BCG and MCC Matrices
49 Developing Strategy

Flexible working

Using methods of working that
cut across established lines,
and old grades and structures

34 Flexible and Self-Managed
    Teams
39 Coaching
15–23 Learning models

Information systems

Designing or changing company
or departmental systems for
gathering, transmitting and
storing information

35 Team Briefing
67 Systems Modelling

Investors in People

A Government-sponsored
scheme which defines effective
procedures for developing staff

58 The Learning Organization
51 Winning Companies
52 Corporate Culture
37–38 Training models
15–23 Learning models

The learning organization

Creating or maintaining a
flexible organization that helps
its members to learn and adapt
continuously to new
circumstances

58 The Learning Organization
50 Excellence Models
51 Winning Companies
15–23 Learning models
34 Flexible and Self-Managed
   Teams

Marketing

Matching goods and services
the company can produce to
the needs of customers

56 The Marketing Mix
55 Competitive Strategy
53 Product Life Cycle
62 Links with Customers
63 The Customer Concept

**New product or service
   development**

Innovation of products or
services to appeal to customer
needs

13 Creativity
12 Thinking Hats
51 Winning Companies
53 Product Life Cycle
60 BCG and MCC Matrices
44 Common Ground
56 The Marketing Mix

Promotion/advertising

Publicizing products or
services or the organization
itself to customers

56 The Marketing Mix
29–30 Motivation models
44 Common Ground
42 Process Model of Persuasion

Recruitment and selection

Appointing people to posts
within the company

36 Person Specification
6 Personality and Psychometrics
15 Learning Needs Analysis

Quality

Maintaining and improving
the quality of goods and services,
as a key to competitiveness

64 Achieving Quality
63 The Customer Concept
66 Project Management
67 Systems Modelling

Re-engineering

Analysing and improving
the processes of production

67 Systems Modelling
65 Trade-Offs
70 Failure and Prevention Costs

Reorganization

Changing the patterns of
responsibility and authority
within an organization –
usually creating new posts
and new systems

50 Excellence Models
51 Winning Companies
61 Downsizing
58 The Learning Organization
31 Theory X and Theory Y
34 Flexible and Self-Managed
   Teams
45 Eight Steps to Organizational
   Change

Strategic alliances

Forging agreements to work
together with partner
organizations, often to deliver
complementary products
and services

41–48 Change models
60 BCG and MCC Matrices
52 Corporate Culture

Strategic thinking

Developing an overall perspective
and plan for an organization that
takes into account the key market,
resource, political and cultural
factors

49 Developing Strategy
50–61 Strategic models

Team building	32 Team Working
	33 Team Roles
Developing a group of people	26 Leadership Styles
into an effective interdependent	25 Action-Centred Leadership
unit	37 Skills Grids
	1 Assertive Behaviour
	3 Life Positions
	14 Circles of Influence
	34 Flexible and Self-Managed Teams

Training and development	15–23 Learning models
	36 Person Specification
Improving the knowledge and	37–39 Training models
skills of people within the	
organization to meet the job	
demands of the future	

THE MANAGEMENT STANDARDS

The British Government has supported the development of National Occupational Standards since 1981 and the publication of the New Training Initiative by the Department of Employment. Standards are expressions of what a person is expected to be able to achieve if they are to be effective in a job role, and they are the basis of vocational qualifications in the UK.

National standards for managers were first developed in 1988–90 by the Management Charter Initiative. Standards to cover managers at all levels, from first-line supervisors to senior executives and board members, were available from 1993, and then subsequently revised and updated between 1995 and 1997. We were closely involved in the development of the first Management Standards, and have remained involved in various projects to implement and evaluate them ever since.

The 1997 Standards divide the manager's role into four core areas, as did the 1990 originals, with the addition of specialist areas on the management of energy, quality and projects. The following tables are designed to be of use to anyone using the Standards for their own development, or the development of others. They show what we think are the main links between the core Standards and the models in this book – or, to put it another way, where the models in this book can help someone to achieve the level of performance described in the Standards.

The Standards are expressed in a very summarized form in these tables. They are Crown Copyright, and a complete set can be obtained from the Management Charter Initiative.

The four core areas are:

A Manage Activities
B Manage Resources
C Manage People
D Manage Information

A Manage Activities

Originally described as Manage Operations, this area concerns the role of producing services and goods to meet customer requirements.

A1–3 Manage activities to meet customer requirements	8 SMART 9–10 Time Management models 24 Leaders and Managers 27 The Functions of Management 28 The Outputs of Management 62–70 Achieving Results models
A4–5 Improve and change work activities	41–48 Change models 62–70 Achieving Results models
A6 Review the operating environment	54 PEST Analysis 69 SWOT Analysis 37 Skills Grids
A7 Establish strategies for the organization	49–61 Strategy models 24 Leaders and Managers 45, 46, 48 Change models
A8 Evaluate and improve overall performance	49–61 Strategy models

B Manage Resources

Originally this area was known as Manage Finance.

B1–B5 Manage resources, including finance, property, supplies and materials	67 Systems Modelling 70 Failure and Prevention Costs

C Manage People

This has always been the largest area of the standards, reflecting its prominence in the work of most managers.

C1–3 Manage and develop yourself	1–23 Self-awareness, personal effectiveness and self-development models
C4–6 Develop productive relationships	3 Life Positions 29–31 Motivation models 32, 33 Team models 46 Networks, Coalitions and Change 47 Political Skills for Managers 48 Stakeholder Analysis
C7–8 Recruitment and selection	36 Person Specification 15 Learning Needs Analysis 37 Skills Grids
C9–11 Develop teams and individuals	8 SMART 15–23 Learning models 37–39 Training models 32, 33, 34 Team models
C12–14 Lead teams and individuals	24 Leaders and Managers 25 Action-Centred Leadership 26 Leadership Styles 28 The Outputs of Management 29–31 Motivation models 32–35 Team models

| C15–17 Discipline, dismissal, redeployment and redundancies | 29 Motivation – the Process
40 Modifying Behaviour
3 Life Positions |

D Manage Information

There are overlaps between all areas of the Standards, perhaps nowhere so obvious as in this role. The information that managers collect, analyse and discuss is about activities, resources and people – the subjects of the previous three groups. Most of the models in this book are about viewing the world in different ways – and are therefore at the heart of shaping and managing information. Because of this, it is tempting to say that all the models are relevant to this role, and none are more relevant than others. We have resisted that temptation, and make some suggestions below, with the caution that some readers may find other models equally relevant.

| D1–4 and 6 Gather information, advise others, hold meetings | 8 SMART
9 Time Management
12 Thinking Hats
13 Creativity
54 PEST Analysis
41 Force Field Analysis
69 SWOT Analysis
67 Systems Modelling
68 Fishbone Analysis
70 Failure and Prevention Costs
48 Stakeholder Analysis
37 Skills Grids
62 Links with Customers
46 Networks, Coalitions and Change
42 Process Model of Persuasion
32, 33 Team models
44 Common Ground |
| D5 Establish information systems | 67 Systems Modelling
35 Team Briefing |

REFERENCES

The Management Standards are available from the Management Charter Initiative, Russell Square House, 10–12 Russell Square, London WC1B 5BZ. Tel: 44 (0) 171 872 9000. The development of the Management Standards has been supported by the Department for Education and Employment.

For the development of Occupational Standards, see Mansfield, B., and Mitchell, L., *Towards a Competent Workforce*, Gower, 1996.

Postscript

We hope you have found the models in this book interesting and useful. We offer here a final model, one that is still in an early stage of development. It is about the process of learning to use mental models.

Models 17 (Learning Cycle), 20 (Double Loop Learning), 21 (Developing Competence) and 22 (Learning Curve) all have a contribution to make to the understanding of this process – and in some ways what we have identified is simply a set of descriptions for points on the learning curve. Not all learning curves are the same, of course, and what may take one person hours or months to grasp, another person may understand in moments. So the following levels are not necessarily a sequence of stages that people follow. And, like all learning curves, there is no guarantee that an individual will continue to progress their ability. Indeed, for some people the lower levels can represent terminal points.

At level 1, I can remember (some of) the words in a model. What are the five stages of Maslow's hierarchy? The four parts of the marketing mix? The seven S's of configuration? I may struggle to remember these details.

At level 2, I can apply the main parts of the model when prompted, or in obvious situations. If we are rescheduling a meeting, or if someone mentions time management, I can talk about importance and urgency (see model 10). If discussions reach a stalemate, with neither side willing to budge, I may think of force field analysis. I am often using parts of the models as labels, however (and sometimes making mistakes about the specific terms), and they are adding little to my ability to handle situations.

At level 3 I am applying the model on my own initiative in appropriate situations. I am beginning to use the model to predict reactions – rather than just as a framework for explaining them after the event. I am still learning how to use the model as well as how to understand the situation, so I still make mistakes, but I am improving my performance by using the model. This approximates to the state of conscious competence in model 21.

At level 4 I can identify and explain a wide range of implications of the model, resolve conflicts between theory and practice, and develop and adapt the model as required to my own situation. Some models may become a natural, internalized framework for understanding events, such that I may have difficulty remembering a time before I used them.

We hope with some of the models in this book you will progress to at least level 3, and perhaps with a smaller number to the degree of use and understanding represented by level 4.

Index